IMAGES
of America

DOWNTOWN
PATERSON

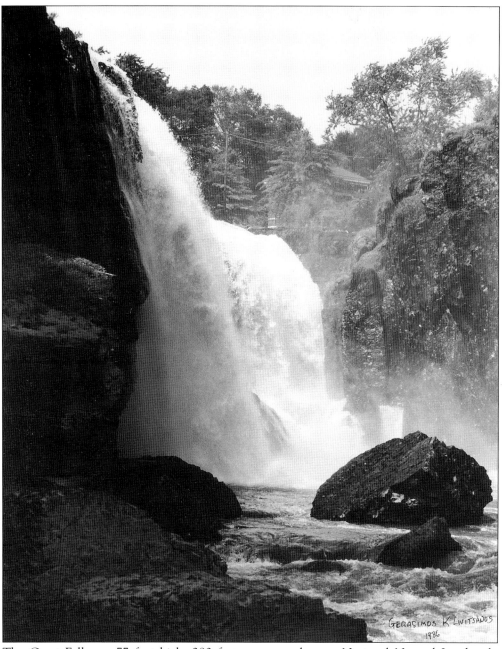
The Great Falls are 77 feet high, 280 feet across, and are a National Natural Landmark. (By G.K. Livitsanos, Courtesy Paterson Museum.)

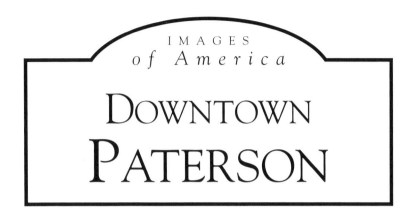

Images of America
Downtown Paterson

Edited by June Avignone

Copyright © 1999 by June Avignone
ISBN 978-0-7385-6323-7

Published by Arcadia Publishing
Charleston SC, Chicago IL, Portsmouth NH, San Francisco CA

Printed in the United States of America

Library of Congress Catalog Card Number: 2008927250

For all general information contact Arcadia Publishing at:
Telephone 843-853-2070
Fax 843-853-0044
E-mail sales@arcadiapublishing.com
For customer service and orders:
Toll-Free 1-888-313-2665

Visit us on the Internet at www.arcadiapublishing.com

Cover Image: Alfonso Torre's fruit and vegetable store, located at 43 Cross Street (now Cianci Street), is shown here *c.* 1920. Alfonso stands with his children, Mildred and Arthur, as his wife, Mary, peers out the store window. Mary and Alfonso are the maternal grandparents of Passaic County Historian Edward A. Smyk. (Courtesy Passaic County Historical Society.)

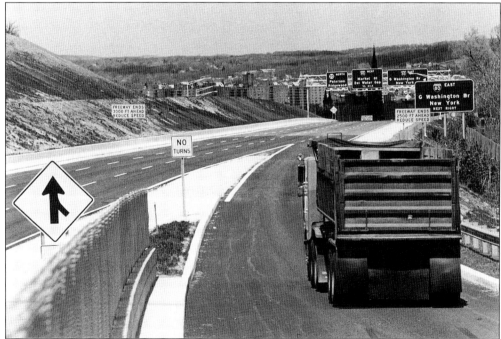

You are entering Paterson, New Jersey. Located 11 miles from New York City, it is 8.36 square miles in area, with a population of 150,000. (By Michael R. Spozarsky, Courtesy Paterson Museum.)

Contents

A Place Like Paterson *by June Avignone*   7

1. Beginnings of Silk City *by Candace Pryor*   11

2. Pride in Labor *by Steve Golin*   23

3. Main Street of Yesteryear *by Edward A. Smyk*   41

4. At the Movies *by Tom Carroll DeBlasio*   61

5. In Paterson *by Mark Hillringhouse*   73

Acknowledgments   96

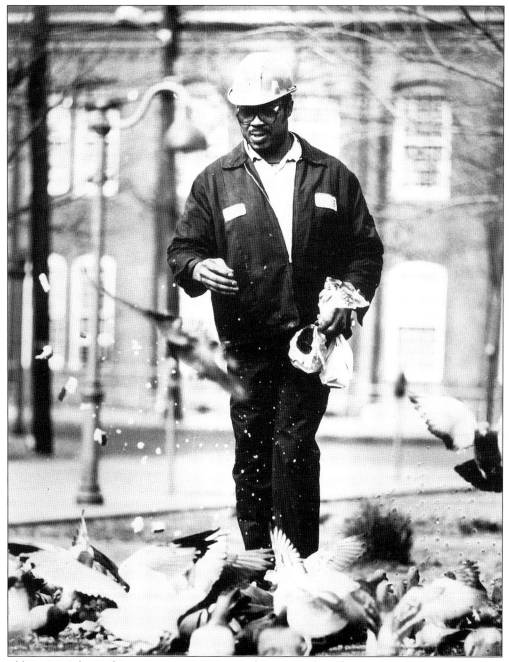

Eldon "Big John" Johnson, a maintenance mechanic at Fabricolor Dyes and Pigments on Van Houten Street, feeds the pigeons every day at noon in the park on Cianci Street. (By David Greedy, Courtesy *North Jersey Herald & News*.)

A Place Like Paterson

Ironies compose the complexities that form Paterson, the first planned industrial city of the United States. Ironies compose what is found in the history of its rich past, and the daily realities of its waking present. All of this must be raked through somehow whenever the question is asked and, it seems, the question is asked often: *What happened to Paterson?*

Some say it was the malls, those indoor suburban wonderlands with fountains, bubble elevators, and everything you could possibly want to buy on the planet. Buy what you can afford, or can't with plastic, then go with packages to a Starbuck's Cafe inside the mega-bookstore beneath fluorescent lights to sip Grande Decaf Mocha cappuccinos, before walking back out to the vast, dark parking lot in the middle of sobering highways. All of this making the external walking of a city street—in the elements of foreign accents mixed with rain and snow and sunshine in the whirling, un-sanitized theater of the absurd along its pavements—an uncalled for accessory.

There was once a majestic downtown here with a Main Street to be rivaled by the sterile, internal highway plazas—those new and improved hearts of our worlds. So be it. This city's Main Street is not alone in its nighttime desolation.

Some say it was an exodus for the American Dream of a house away from the growing whispers of fear, an exchange of a seemingly escapable diversity for a separating lawn and picket fence. With it all, the growing need for many to get in the car and drive to the corner mailbox or Home Depot, then to some corporate restaurant chain on the highway, only miles away from the city with "the problems."

Those with knowledge of history or an interest in memory say that the reasons for imbalances in a city can be traced back even further, here in Paterson to a continuance of a spirit that began when a group of rich men harnessed the Great Falls for profit, founding Paterson as a corporation instead of chartering it as a city in 1792. Industry came to the land of the Lenape Indians and silk became the never-ending fruit, or so it was planned. But there was a catch. The individual spirits of people, viewed as part of the machinery, were radically alive.

Some have said that a "Renaissance" of Paterson's Historic District would help the proverbial Silk City, here in the neighborhood with the brick mills once powered by the Great Falls, where thousands of men, women, and children from diverse backgrounds once worked. Joining forces with the Industrial Workers of the World (IWW) in 1913, they fought for rights, like the eight-hour workday, against the politically and commercially powerful. In short, they fought a revolution, against great odds, that helped bring us rights we still benefit from today.

The eventual decline of the once plentiful mills took jobs with them, unraveling the silk lining of an incendiary past not easily forgotten, in need of solutions not easily found. After years of watching some of the vacant historic buildings burn down, some say a kind of a

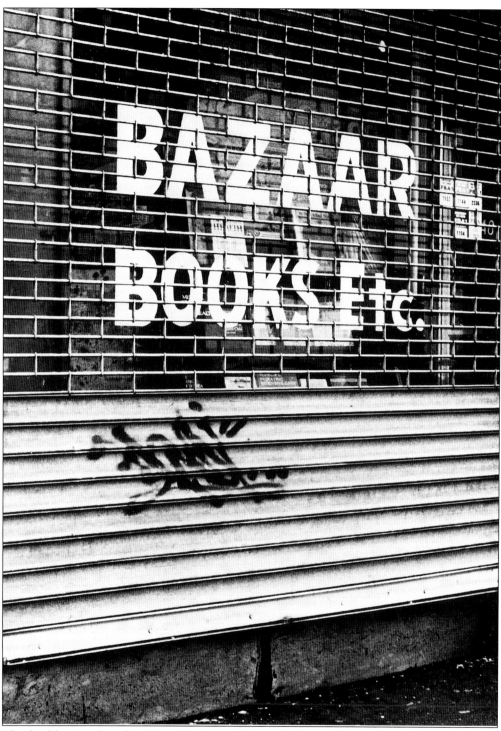

The final bastion for eclectic book lovers was Bazaar Books on Ellison Street, which closed its doors in 1996. (By John Munson, Courtesy *North Jersey Herald & News*.)

"rebirth" may be coming here after all. Current developers, albeit under more than appealing deals for themselves, have restored or are planning to restore the burned-out shells of these mills and other properties into housing, and more development plans seem to be waiting in politically backed wings. In the end, despite some sudden public opposition raised at stormy council meetings, who can truly progressively argue against more affordable housing? In our fragmented philosophical times, any means seem to justify that end.

But what will even more people do here at night? The city of 150,000 lacks a hometown daily newspaper to watchdog corruption or report with direct insight on its people, places, and needs. The abundant go-go bars, where women do just about anything for a dollar, remain the main source of nightly entertainment. There is not one movie theater left in Paterson. No youth center is planned for the area or the city at large, although one is desperately needed.

So some wisely ask: Is there an identifiable, balanced, overall working plan for Silk City's Historic District that truly and aggressively takes the individual needs of a community under development to heart? Indeed, Paterson has a powerful past, and with it, a pervading continuance of special interests of which we deny ourselves a full holistic recognition, despite the much-touted "history" here.

Some say it is not a "positive thing" to sling arrows, but Cupid did, and besides, what can be the real danger of asking what happened to the quality of life of a place like Paterson? To be able to walk to a theater again or a bookstore along its streets; to walk in safety at night; to again see the beautiful turn-of-the-century architecture of historic buildings downtown, Grand Dames now scathed over with plastic Day-Glo facades that read "99¢ Dream" and "99¢ Reality." Paterson is the perverse product of an epic corporate experiment, a perpetual magnifying lens into complicated, ongoing class struggles.

Yet, within the struggle, some will say there are still diamonds to be found here among the shards of glass on these streets. They may appear in the form of a cappuccino made by an old Italian man at the Roma Club on Cianci Street; the Peruvian lady with the beautiful, dark-eyed little girl in the luncheonette on Van Houten, which has the best rice and beans around; or the big man with the gentle heart, originally from South Carolina, who works at the dye factory and feeds the pigeons everyday at noon in the park with the statue of Lou Costello, across from the restored mill I call home.

For there are those who say that the spirit of the individual has always dwelled here, in spite of the still-convenient Silk City corporate image that follows Paterson around like a haunted public relations mirage. As William Carlos Williams wrote in his classic poem *Paterson*, "A man in himself is a city, beginning, seeking, achieving and concluding his life in ways which the various aspects of a city may embody." To defend the heart of the city is in the natural light of that spirit.

Some say it was the malls. Some say it is best to remember that nothing costs 99 cents, with tax. Some say our cities, in reality as well as our dreams, reveal our true hearts at work. And that it may, ironically, serve us all well to take a closer look.

—June Avignone

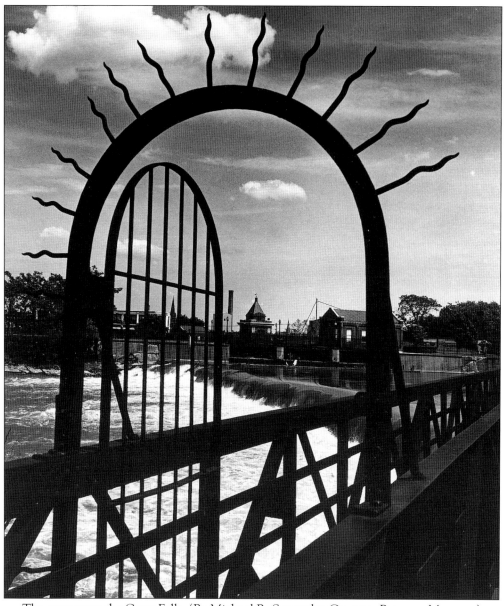

The gateway to the Great Falls. (By Michael R. Spozarsky, Courtesy Paterson Museum.)

Since the young Alexander Hamilton had thrilled to the sight of the Totowa Falls and saw in this heedless power the center of American industry, the Falls had thrashed and plunged and thrown up mists, and, though the harnessed flow had been diminished by the three millraces, the Falls remained an essentially wild thing at Paterson's heart, a distillation of all that is furious and accidental and overwhelming in nature, a gem of pure ruinous uncaring around which the aching generations came and went. The Falls had been here when only the Leni-Lenapes had stood rapt before such careless grandeur and would be here when Paterson had sunk back into a crooked valley of brick, rubble, and rusted iron.

—John Updike, from *In the Beauty of the Lilies*
(Copyright 1997, reprinted by permission of Alfred A. Knopf Inc., New York.)

One

BEGINNINGS OF SILK CITY

In many ways, the early history of Paterson as an industrial enterprise reflects the beginnings of the new nation: the participation of a select few in an evolutionary atmosphere of trial and error, success and failure, and, in the end, the emergence of the individual as a necessary participant in the economic and political process.

When the Dutch negotiated trinkets and blankets for the area called Ackquackanonk with the local Lenape Indians in the late 17th century, they had no idea that the peaceful farming community would eventually become the center of planned industry. In 1791, Alexander Hamilton, secretary of the treasury and the leading proponent of Federalist ideology, presented his Report on Manufactures to Congress. It proposed that the new country begin its own system of commercial development, and stressed the need to produce American goods, such as cotton, thread, and paper. This argument for a strong national government was in direct opposition to the agrarian republicanism espoused by Thomas Jefferson and James Madison. Congress did not adopt the plan, but many specific measures from the report were enacted as early as the following year. More importantly, Hamilton and the Federalist's overall vision of the importance of industry proved invaluable in the acceptance of the plan for Paterson.

New Jersey Governor William Paterson, a leading Federalist and supporter of Hamilton's vision of national government, signed the legislation creating the Society for Establishing Useful Manufactures (SUM) in 1791. The New Jersey charter granted SUM control of the waterways, and exemption from all taxes for 10 years (and all taxes except state-imposed taxes after that.) The sponsors—leading politicians, wealthy capitalists, and speculators—named their town after the governor. The concept of an industrial city came to fruition in 1792 on the banks of Great Falls, when the population was only about 50. William Duer, a wealthy New York speculator and an intimate of Hamilton's, was elected the first president of the SUM's board of directors. The board established committees for making land appropriations, building factories and housing, and recruiting skilled workers from New York City and Europe.

From 1791 to 1796, the society had little to show for its efforts. William Duer was cited for misappropriation of $10,000 and landed in New York City debtor's prison as the result of failed business dealings during the Financial Panic of 1792. An additional $50,000 of the SUM's limited capital designated for mechanics and equipment from England and Scotland was lost. Mismanagement, scandal, labor shortages, and the lack of new investors prompted the SUM to discontinue its own operations and lease or sell their facilities to individuals.

In 1795, English immigrant John Clark leased part of the failing SUM's Paterson Cotton Mill to establish the state's first machine shop. Nearly every successful commercial enterprise before 1850 was run by men trained by Clark or one of his disciples.

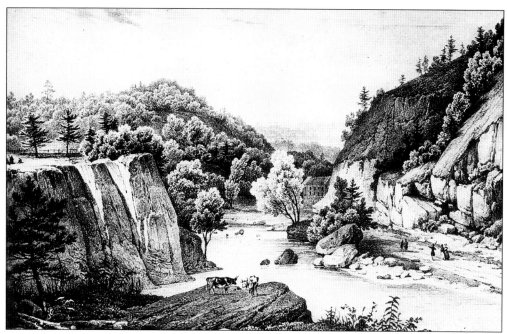

The Lenape, or the "original people," knew the Great Falls primarily as a camping and fishing site. They called it "Totowa," which means "to sink or be forced down beneath the waters." As depicted in these early-18th-century prints, the first white men gazed at the natural wonder in the 17th century, most likely following the settlement of Newark in 1666, when hunters or land prospectors wandered up the Passaic River and returned to tell about it. The Lenapes were called "Old Women" by other tribes because of their peaceful nature. Ultimately, the Lenapes were eliminated from Passaic County and all the state. (Courtesy Paterson Museum.)

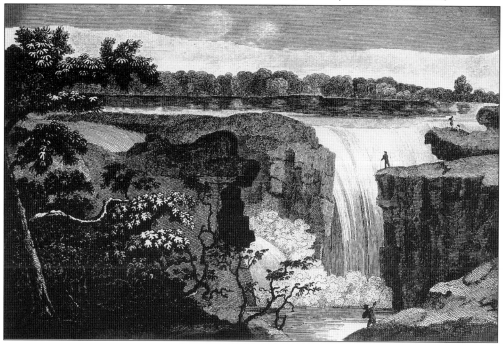

The SUM also turned to New England for experienced administrators. To address the city's struggles, the corporation induced Peter Colt, secretary of the treasury in Connecticut, to resign in 1793. As Paterson's superintendent of works, Colt succeeded Major Pierre Charles L'Enfant, the engineer-architect of Washington, D.C., who had drawn the original raceway plans for Paterson. A friend of Hamilton's, the French planner said his design for Paterson would surpass anything yet seen in the United States, and that he would make it the largest, most elegant city in the nation. But L'Enfant's plan did not take into consideration the rocky terrain of the area, nor a canal to conduct water for power, and his extravagance exceeded the limited capital of the SUM. Consequently, the SUM fired him two years later, marking the end of comprehensive city planning in Paterson.

The SUM did not dissolve, but remained inactive until 1814. It was the individual interests of the pragmatic Colt family that salvaged the SUM's weak beginnings. In actuality, whoever controlled the SUM dominated Paterson. By 1816 the Colts owned 1,991 of the organization's 2,620 available shares. Peter Colt's sons were also influential in the development of Paterson as an industrial center. Roswell Colt, who was instrumental in rejuvenating the SUM in 1814, served as governor of the society until his death in 1856; John Colt is credited with the cotton sailcloth and was a major supplier to the U.S. Navy; and Christopher Colt first made silk in Paterson. From another branch of the family, Samuel Colt invented the Colt revolver. He first tried to raise money for a factory by roaming the East Coast with a portable magic show. Finally, finding backers in Paterson in 1835, he built the Gun Mill. It was Peter's sister Sarah who began the first Sunday school in New Jersey in 1794.

When the Colt silk mill failed after two years of production it was sold to George Murray, who employed John Ryle, a 22 year old from England. Ryle's knowledge of the textile industry proved invaluable and he was soon made a partner. He revolutionized the industry by inventing the process to wind silk on spools and made the first silk flag. John Ryle bought out his partner and by the Civil War the "Father of the Silk Industry" employed 500 people.

Innovation was also evident in the spirit of individuals like Charles Kinsey, who patented a machine for making paper in one continuous roll. Kinsey did not leave his cotton mill to pursue paper production and, like other cotton makers, the business failed during the Panic of 1816. John Phillip Holland, an Irish immigrant and math teacher at St. John's Parochial School, built the first practical submarine. Barely large enough to hold one man, the boat had its first run in the Passaic River on May 22, 1878. With the success of the *Holland I*, the inventor was able to persuade funders to put up money for larger, more advanced vessels.

Thomas Rogers moved from Connecticut to Paterson in 1812. Rogers was very successful as a mechanic and engineer and soon retired, but he was lured out of retirement to make iron bridges for the expanding railroad lines. In 1835, Rogers was asked to re-assemble a locomotive from England. Convinced that he could do better, he built his own locomotive, the *Sandusky*, and gave the industry its start in Paterson in 1837. By 1860, Paterson was home to three locomotive factories; only Philadelphia could claim to produce more locomotives.

Hamilton's conception of an industrial nation would change the fabric of American life. The industrialists fought for a political presence in a state legislature still essentially run by rural interests. As a result of political pressure, county lines were redrawn and Passaic County was carved from Essex and Bergen Counties in 1837. By 1860, Paterson had grown in size with a population of almost 20,000. The population growth and immigration created social problems: labor inequality, the need for education, housing, and city services, which would be addressed—to some extent—by 19th-century reform movements.

While Paterson's corporate beginnings were fueled by wealthy capitalists, it remains increasingly important to remember that it was the individual inventor, shopkeeper, machinist, and business entrepreneur who would become an integral part of the city's economic process.

—Candace Pryor

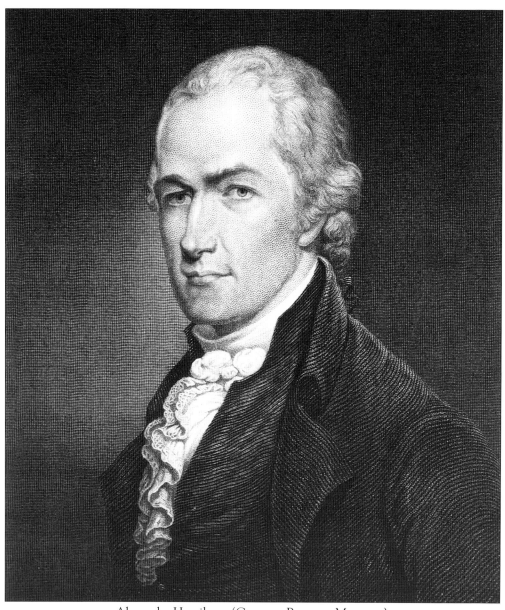

Alexander Hamilton. (Courtesy Paterson Museum.)

Paterson may well be the most instructive city in the United States for exploring the roots of the American urban crisis. It was, of course, not meant to become a city whose main thoroughfare is edged by tenements and the scene of bi-monthly welfare traffic jams. It was designed to become, among other things, the largest and most elegant city in the United States, a "national manufactory," and a majestic symbol of American power... In the singular vision of industrial might, empire and corporate power that inspired the city's beginnings, it might be said that the future of the United States, and, more specifically, the future of all American cities was essentially decided.

—Christopher Norwood, from *About Paterson*
(Copyright 1974, E.P. Dutton & Co., Inc, New York; used with permission of the author.)

It was Hamilton's Report on Manufactures, submitted to Congress on December 5, 1791, that served as the catalyst for the creation of the Society of Establishing Useful Manufactures (SUM). To the right is the official SUM seal, which helped promote industry as the angel of progress. (Courtesy Paterson Museum.)

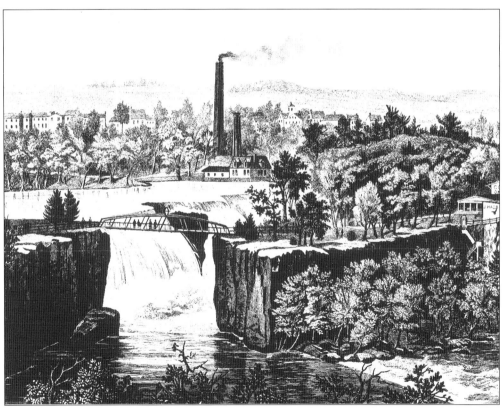

This 18th-century rendering of the Great Falls by J.L. Giles depicts the transformation of the area's riverside farming community into an industrial center. (Courtesy Paterson Museum.)

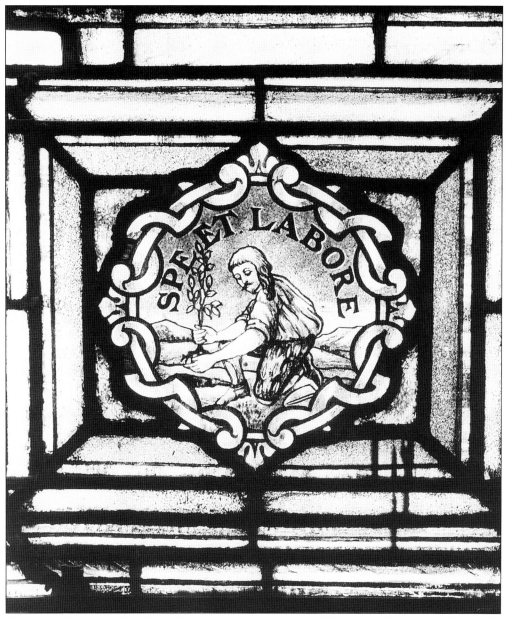

The coat of arms for the City of Paterson was adopted in 1869 during the term of John Ryle as mayor. Known as the father of the silk industry in the United States, Ryle was active in the business of silk manufacturing when he held the office of mayor. He suggested the idea and the motto "Spe et Labore" (Hope and Labor). The design is of a man planting a mulberry bush from which silkworms feed, representing the only branch of the silk industry's manufacturing process that did not exist in the city. An effort was made to cultivate the tree, but because of the climate the experiment failed. (Courtesy Paterson Museum.)

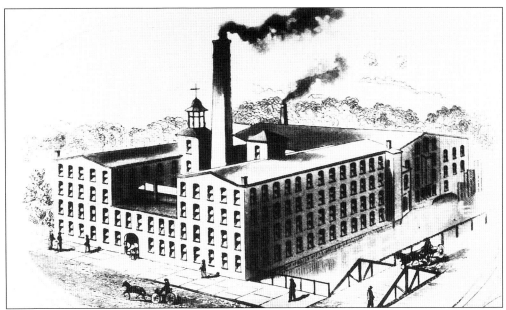

These early lithographs of the Essex Mill (top) and the Harmony and Industry Mills (bottom) were depicted in renderings from the *History of Industrial Paterson* (1880) by L.R. Trumbull. The Essex on Mill Street began exclusively as a yarn factory in 1804, but during the War of 1812 it was converted to a cotton mill. The Essex Mill, along with the Phoenix Mill, built in 1815 on Van Houten Street, was renovated in the 1980s by a private developer to serve as a federally subsidized housing project for artists. The Industry Mill on Van Houten Street began as a sawmill and was later changed to a cotton mill in 1830. The Industry Silk Mill was built in front of the Industry Cotton Mill in 1879; the Harmony Mill, located next to the Industry Mill, was originally a small wooden structure built by Squire Smith in 1822. Destroyed by fires in the 1980s, only portions of these mills remain today. (Courtesy Paterson Museum.)

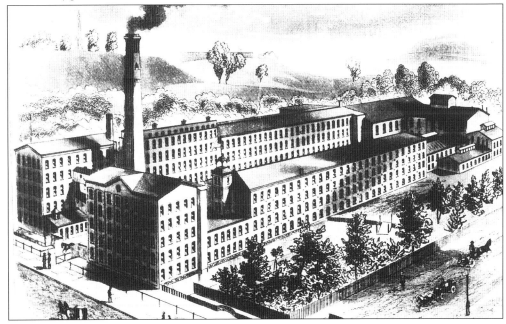

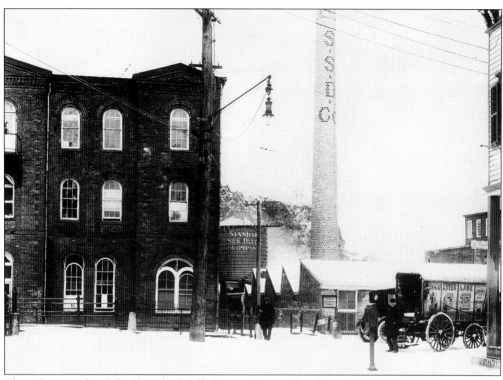

This photograph of the Standard Silk Dyers Co. on Van Houten Street was taken c. 1916. Only a small portion of this mill stands today; the rest was destroyed by fire. (Courtesy Paterson Museum.)

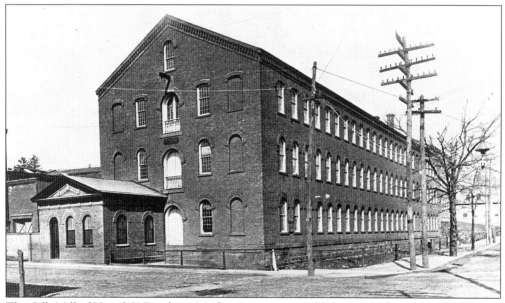

The Silk Mill of Hamil & Booth on Market Street was established by Robert Hamil and James Booth in 1857. Both men worked as superintendents in the silk industry for John Ryle prior to forming their partnership in 1855. The building was destroyed by fire in 1983. (Courtesy Paterson Museum.)

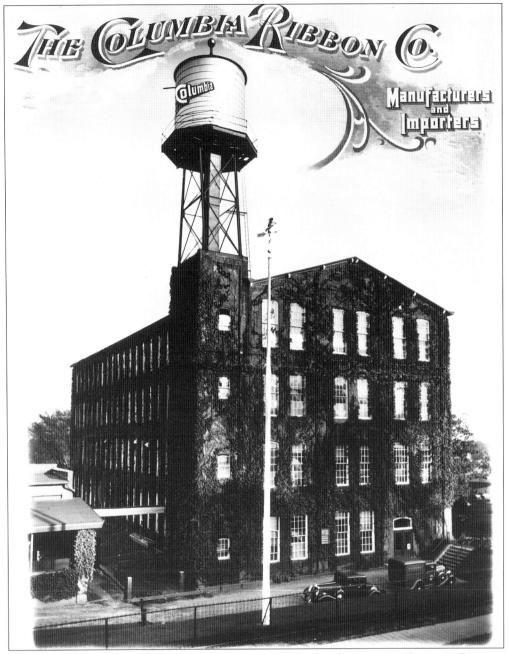

The Columbia Ribbon Company was located on Railroad Avenue. (Courtesy Paterson Museum.)

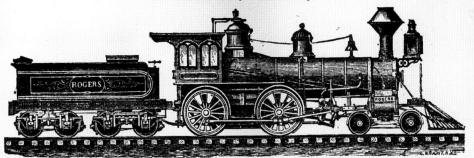

By 1854, the firm of Rogers, Ketchum, and Grosvenor had made 554 engines, and by 1873 it was producing one engine every second day on an assembly line. Rogers' son Jacob inherited the locomotive works (below) in 1856. After a huge fire in 1879, Jacob built the structure still standing on the corner of Market and Spruce Streets. Together, three locomotive manufacturing companies—the Rogers Locomotive Works, the Danforth & Cooke Company, and the Grant Locomotive Company—produced thousands of steam locomotive engines. (Courtesy Paterson Museum.)

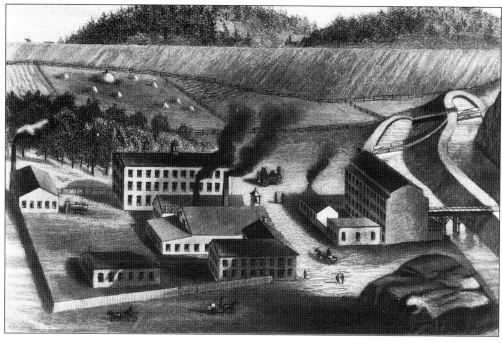

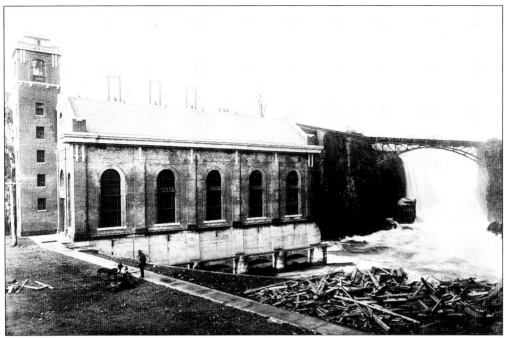

The power of Paterson's waterways was further utilized in 1914 when the Great Falls Hydroelectric Plant was placed into service. The plant generated electricity for manufacturers in the city and its environs for 55 years. The old plant was decommissioned in 1969, but was restored on December 30, 1986. The Federal Department of Energy provided $1.32 million for construction assistance, with the total project cost of $14.5 million met by a private developer. The station has an installed capacity of 10,950 kilowatts, the entire output of which was purchased by PSE&G. (Courtesy Paterson Museum.)

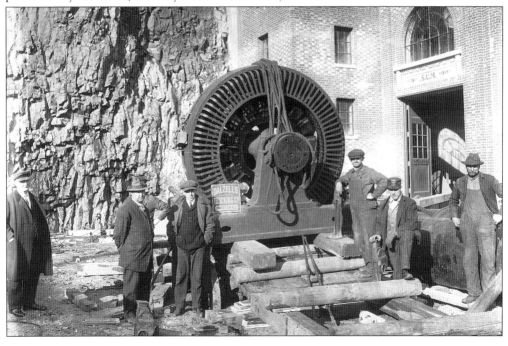

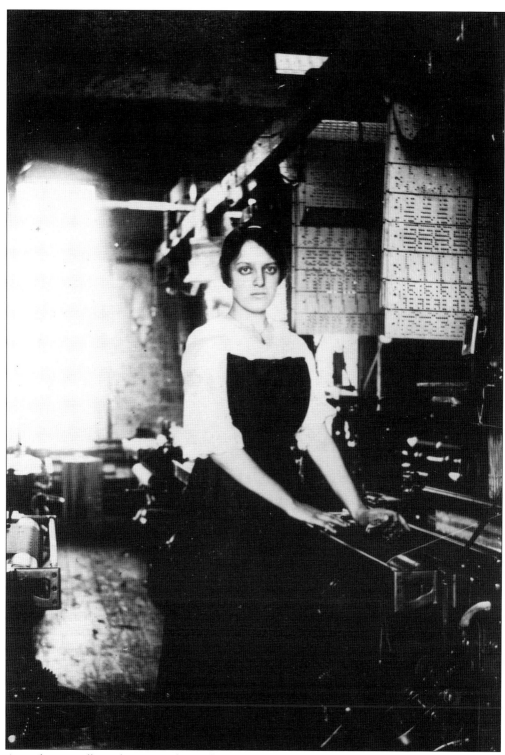
An unknown silk worker poses alongside a jacquard loom in the early 20th century. (Courtesy American Labor Museum.)

Two

Pride in Labor

Paterson, 100 years ago, was a good city in which to be a worker. Through a system of ward representation, working people had a say in Paterson politics. On many key issues, workers had allies in the middle class. Together, they prevented the richest Patersonians—the big silk manufacturers—from dominating the politics or the culture of Paterson. That's why, in 1890, the manufacturers started building annexes in Pennsylvania, where their workers were easier to control and exploit. In Paterson, you could picket without being harassed by the police. You could strike, as silk weavers did in 1877 and 1894. And you could win.

As a result, weaving was good work, for men and women. The pay averaged more than twice that of unskilled workers, such as a day laborers. Weavers often owned their own homes in Paterson or in Haledon. Women weavers kept their jobs in Paterson even after they got married. Men and women taught their kids how to weave. They did not despise the work, or see themselves as sacrificing so their children could escape Paterson and the mills. Weavers were proud of their skill, of their power, and of their community. Backed by sections of the Paterson middle class, they fought to preserve, improve, and pass on to their children their satisfying way of life. Look at the picture of the Botto House. Botto was a weaver.

It was a different reality for the dye workers. With 300 firms in Paterson, the silk dyeing industry was far more concentrated than silk manufacturing, which was decentralized, with 300 firms in Paterson. Silk dyeing was more of a big business, like Hamilton had in mind when he imagined Paterson. Workers were unskilled. Working conditions were horrible. A dyers' helper could barely live on the salary if the work was regular, which it was not.

However, as the 20th century began, the largest group of workers in Paterson was silk weavers. When they started, and led, the great 1913 strike, they were not struggling to survive. They were struggling, as they always had, to protect their say on the job and the quality of their lives. The two big issues in 1913 were winning the eight-hour day—"eight hours for work, eight hours for sleep, eight hours for pleasure"—and limiting the numbers of looms per weaver.

During the 1913 strike, the weavers reached out to others. They formed a powerful alliance with the unskilled dye workers. They asked the creative democratic union known as the IWW (Industrial Workers of the World) to provide them with logistical support. They sent their kids to stay with Socialists in New York and staged a pageant about their strike in Madison Square Garden, with the help of artists and writers from Greenwich Village. And, as always, they received crucial support from sections of Paterson's middle class, in the form of bread and money.

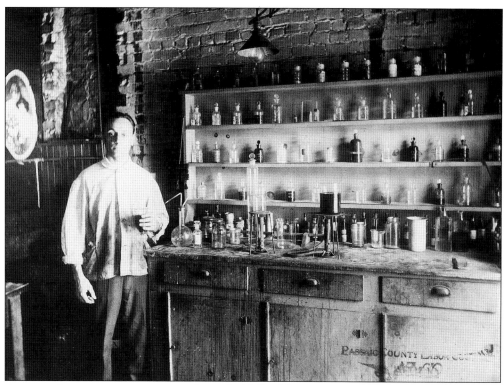
A master dyer prepares pigments in the early 1900s. (Courtesy American Labor Museum.)

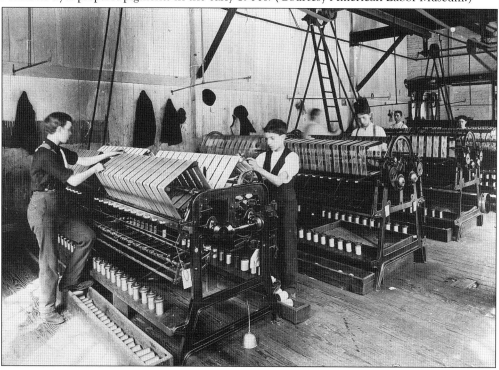
Young boys work in the mills, *c.* 1900. (Courtesy American Labor Museum.)

However, most of their middle-class support now came only from Jews and Italians. Other middle-class Patersonians were running scared. At one time, silk weavers were primarily northern and western Europeans (English, French, and German). The new immigrants, however, were southern and eastern Europeans (Italians and Polish Jews). Prejudices in Paterson and throughout the country were strong against the new immigrants. Seizing the advantage, the manufacturers pointed to the anarchistic ideology of some Italians and to the violent reputation of the IWW as a way to justify a get-tough policy on the new immigrants.

Most middle-class people bought it. Before the strike, they supported the abolition of the ward system, and finally gave the manufacturers the control they wanted. In 1913, for the first time, the manufacturers were able to tell the police and the local court what to do. Strikers were no longer allowed to picket in Paterson. The police arrested and the court sentenced about 2,000 strikers for picketing in 1913. Paterson, which had been a good city for workers, was changing.

Even so, 23,000 strikers held out for five months. From February through June, they shut down the mills and dye houses. Paterson's economy was devastated; it had once featured locomotive and gun manufacturing, but was now dependent solely on silk. Late in the 1913 strike, small merchants got together, driven by desperation, and petitioned the federal government to intervene. It was too little, too late. Having bought into the rising hysteria about immigrants and radicals, Paterson's small businessmen and professionals watched their city become ravaged by class warfare.

The strike ended indecisively, without an eight-hour day, but also without an increase in loom assignments. Silk manufacturers continued to move more and more of their business out of Paterson to Pennsylvania and weavers continued to protest against wage cuts and to strike. In a 1924 strike, the mayor proposed deporting immigrant strikers and was applauded by the local KKK. During the Great Depression, Paterson's dye workers successfully won the right to have a union. The class struggle continued until the coming of synthetics and the Depression closed down the vast majority of silk mills permanently.

Hardly anyone remembers now that Paterson was once such a good place to work that skilled men and women came from all over Europe to share in, and contribute to, Paterson's vibrant working-class culture.

—Steve Golin

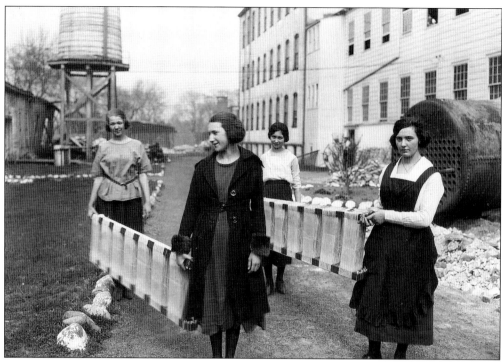
Women silk workers carry linen harnesses, early 1900s. (Courtesy Paterson Museum.)

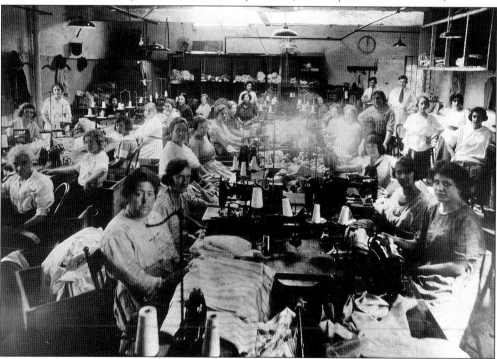
In 1906, these women at the Manhattan Shirt Company on River Street worked a standard 10-hour day. The factory was a source of employment for many Paterson residents for decades. (Courtesy Paterson Museum.)

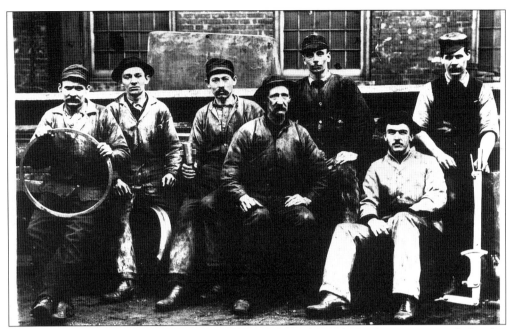

Workers at the Danforth and Cooke Locomotive and Machine Company posed for this photograph around 1890. Shown here are, from left to right, William Forbs, Frank Lovell, Adolph Wold, P. King, William Campbell, Charles D. Cooke, and James Binney. (Courtesy Passaic County Historical Society.)

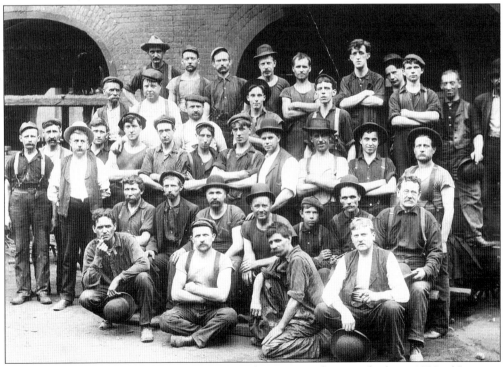

These workers in the Rogers Locomotive shop were photographed c. 1900. (Courtesy Paterson Museum.)

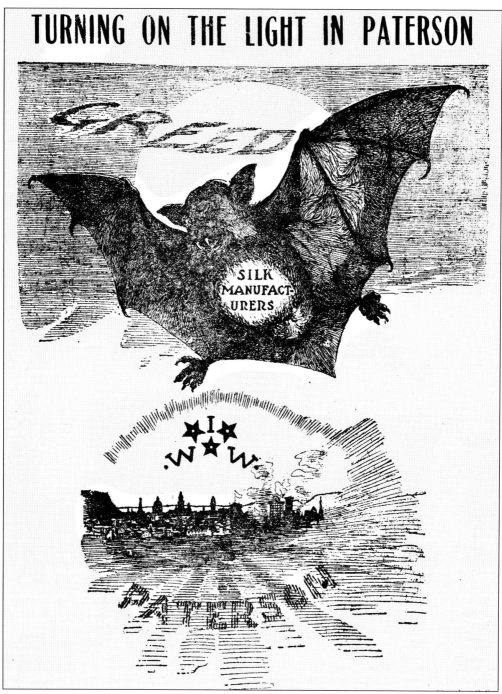

"Turning on the Light in Paterson," an Industrial Workers of the World cartoon, was published in the April 19, 1913 issue of the newspaper *Solidarity*. It depicts the struggle against silk manufactures looming above the efforts of the IWW. The Wobblies, as they were called, wanted to end the class system through democratic and nonviolent techniques of organization, and would actively involve women and immigrants. (Courtesy of Labor and Urban Affairs, Wayne University.)

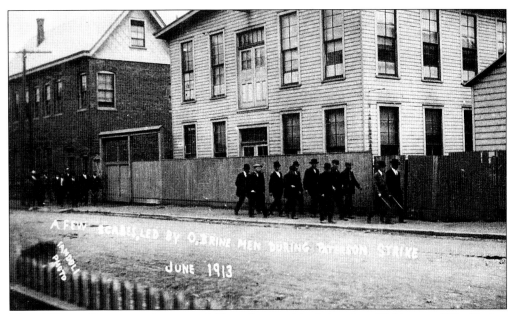

The O'Brien Detective Agency of Newark was hired by the Weidmann Silk Dyeing Company during the 1913 strike. The battle between the detectives and the dyer's helpers epitomized the fierceness of class war in Paterson in 1913. Above, O'Brien detectives, who were often more violent than the police, protect a small group of strikebreakers. (Courtesy American Labor Museum.)

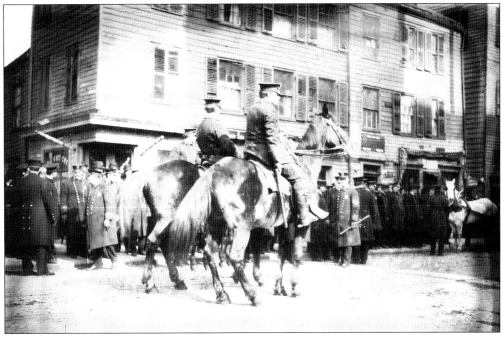

During the 1913 strike, Chief John Bimson's police force arrested strikers for picketing and IWW leaders for being "outside agitators." Eventually strikers were barred by police from Turn Hall, located on Ellison and Cross Streets (now Cianci Street), where they had rallied for meetings and speeches daily. (Courtesy Paterson Museum.)

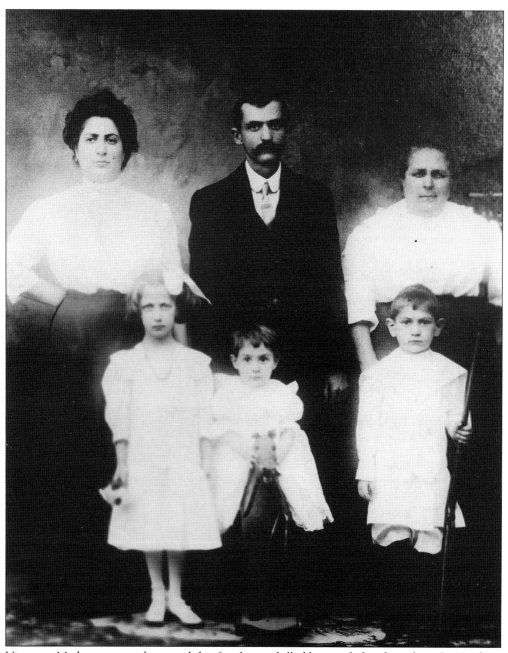
Vincenzo Madonna, seen above with his family, was killed by a strikebreaker whom Dr. Andrew F. McBride, the mayor of Paterson in 1913, had authorized to carry a weapon. (Courtesy American Labor Museum.)

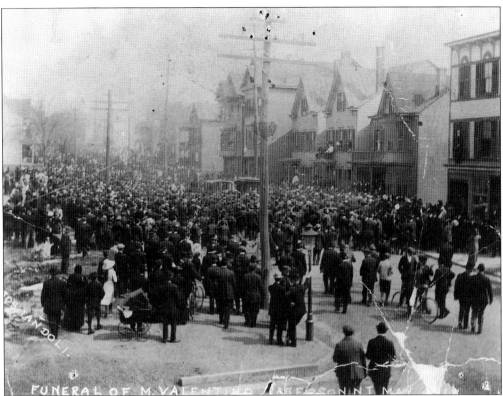

Valentino Modestino was shot to death by an O'Brien detective guarding the Weidmann plant on April 17, 1913, at 6:30 p.m. Modestino, who was not a silk worker, had just come home from his job and was standing on the front stoop of his home in the Riverside section of Paterson. He was watching a confrontation between dyer's helpers and the special detectives as they put a group of strikebreakers in a trolley car. Shots were fired by O'Brien's men to intimidate the strikers and one hit Modestino in the back. His suspected killer, Detective Joseph Cutherton, was arrested after the shooting but never indicted, despite strong evidence against him. Postcards made of Modestino's funeral procession, like the one above, were sold to support relief efforts of the strikers. (Courtesy American Labor Museum.)

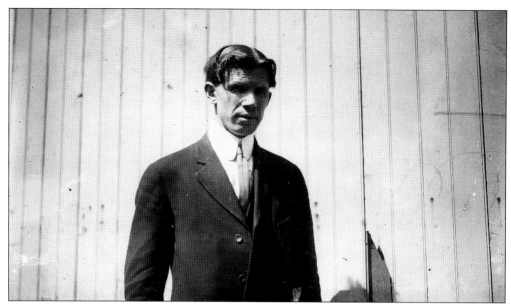

IWW leader Patrick Quinlan arrived late at the February 25, 1913 meeting. Nevertheless, he was later sentenced to a term of two to seven years in state prison in Trenton on the trumped-up charge of inciting violence for a speech that he had not made. He was released in 1916, at which time he left the IWW and returned to work for the Socialist Party. (Courtesy American Labor Museum.)

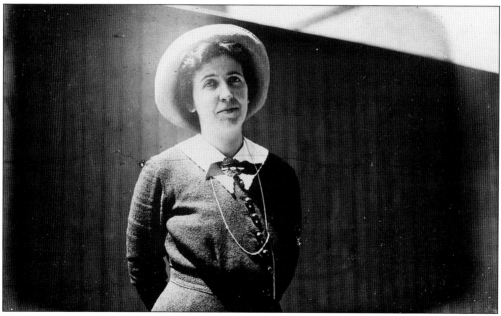

Elizabeth Gurley Flynn, a major IWW leader of the 1913 strike, felt "the rich owned America" and that the Wobblies represented the "ideal spirit" for the country. On February 25, the first day of the 1913 strike, before being arrested by the police, she warned her audience at Turn Hall to guard against being divided by the police and manufactures and not to be "tricked by racial prejudice, for they'll tell you that the Jews are going to work and then they'll tell you that the Italians have gone back to work." (Courtesy American Labor Museum.)

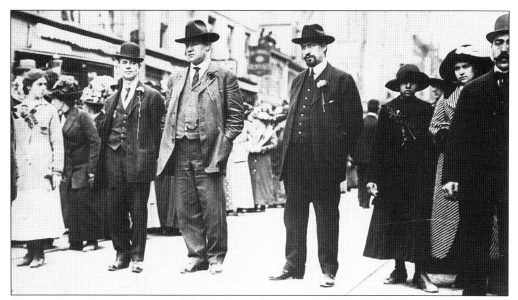

Despite their frequent arrests, Adolph Lessig, William D. ("Big Bill") Haywood, and Carlo Tresca always returned to the streets and halls. In 1913, Lessig, a broad-silk weaver in the David Mill, was heading and organizing silk workers' Local 152. Haywood helped found the IWW in 1905 as a revolutionary alternative to the American Federation of Labor. Tresca, an anarchist, had come to the United States from southern Italy in 1904 as a revolutionary fugitive. (Courtesy American Labor Museum.)

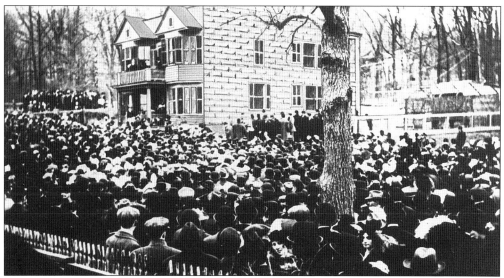

The Haledon home of silk weaver Pietro Botto and his wife, Maria, immigrants from northern Italy, became the new rallying grounds for strikers in 1913 after Mayor McBride barred mass meetings in Paterson. However, Haledon's Socialist mayor, William Bruekmann, welcomed the strikers. Audiences of up to 25,000 would come on Sundays to hear IWW leaders and strike sympathizers, such as Upton Sinclair, Max Eastman, and John Reed, who spoke from the small balcony on Norwood Street. The house, which was placed on the National and State Registers of Historic Sites in 1975, is the site of the American Labor Museum today. (Courtesy American Labor Museum.)

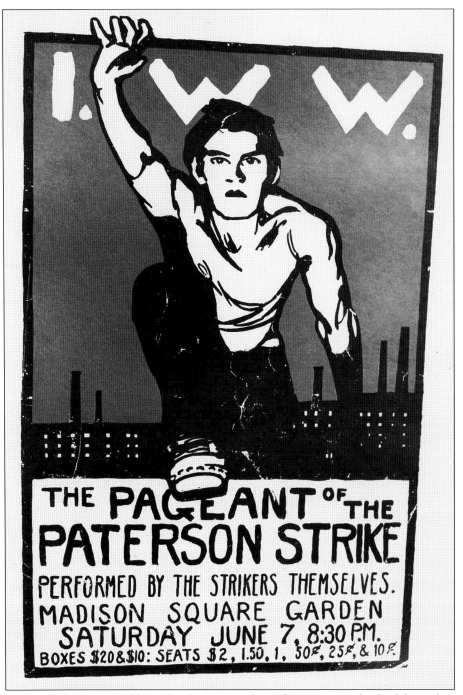

The greatest effort to get publicity for the 1913 strike and raise money for food for strikers was the Pageant of the Paterson Strike held at Madison Square Garden on June 7. In the staged reenactment of the strike itself, Greenwich Village artists and intellectuals joined forces with the labor leaders and a cast of thousands of strikers who played themselves in the pageant. Above is the powerful design by artist Robert Edmund Jones that appeared in advertisements and on the program cover. (Courtesy American Labor Museum.)

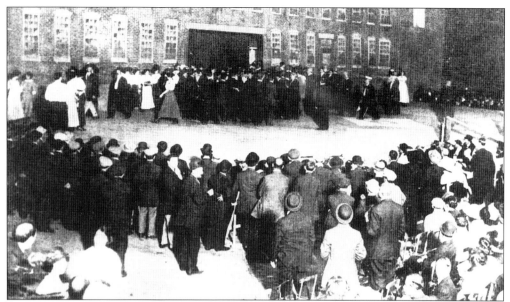

At Madison Square Garden, in front of John Sloan's painting of a giant silk mill, strikers enacted a confrontation with the police in the second episode of the pageant. The audience of 15,000 was overwhelmingly working class. As one reporter from the newspaper *Solidarity* expressed it: "The people on the stage had long forgotten the audience. The audience had long forgotten itself and become the scene." John Sloan, a Socialist, was one of the "Eight Painters" of the realist or Ashcan School in New York. (Courtesy American Labor Museum.)

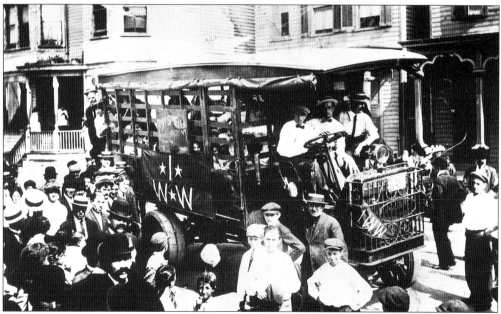

During the hardships of the 1913 strike, children of the strikers facing hunger were sent to live with families in New York willing to take care of them until the strike ended. More than 100 New York families were enlisted by the IWW. On May 1, the first group of 85 children left Paterson. The New York Committee was led by experienced women, such as Elizabeth Gurley Flynn, Margaret Sanger, Dolly Sloan, and Jessie Ashley. (Courtesy American Labor Museum.)

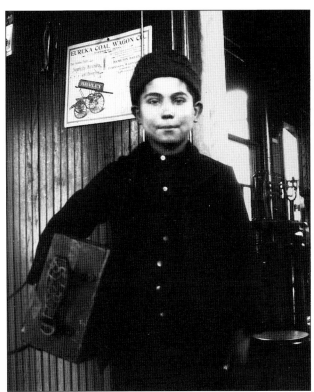

An unidentified shoeshine boy poses for a photographer, c. 1890. (Courtesy Passaic County Historical Society.)

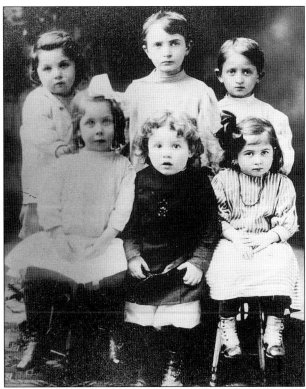

This group of Jewish strikers' children were photographed during the 1913 Strike. (Courtesy American Labor Museum.)

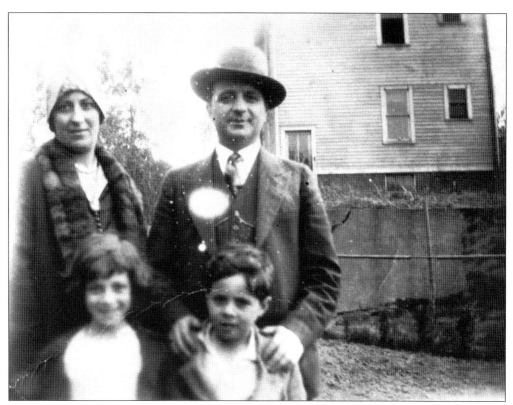

Lifelong Patersonian Josephine Stifano worked in the mills as a child through adulthood. In this family photograph, Josephine stands with her husband, Nicola, an Italian immigrant from Salerno, and two of her four children, Angelina and Victor, by their Brook Street home. Shortly before her death in 1998, Josephine shared the following memories. (Courtesy Victor Stifano.)

    Believe me when I say the whole city was starving, the whole city of Paterson was haunted in 1913. No one was working, everyone was on strike, everyone was hungry. Not like now, no relief, welfare. I was 10 in 1913. We had to leave, my uncle in West Virginia said there was work and we came back to Paterson when I was 12. They say to me, how can you remember? I say, when you had pain, you remember. I started to work in the mills at 12. I didn't use my name. I had to get false working papers. We had no choice. I was working 10 hours a day, six days a week. Any money could help us eat. I worked in the mill across from School Two, a dye house. They had to put me up on a box to work. I would hear the recess bell from the school and cry. I would watch the children playing at the school from the window and cry. I wanted to play with them. The foreman told me I couldn't stand by the window anymore. But the owner heard him once and said let her stand by the window. I learned all I could, all phases. I ended up being a weaver. I was proud of my work. I can remember so clearly, everything so clearly.

—Josephine Stifano
January 30, 1903–July 21, 1998

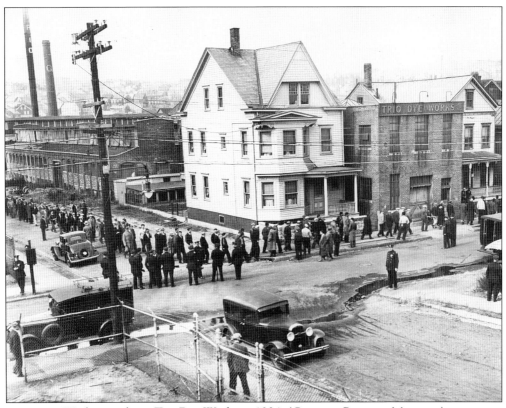

Workers strike at Trio Dye Works in 1934. (Courtesy Paterson Museum.)

Dye House Strike, 1933

When the dye house went on strike in 1933, I was living in an old farmhouse at the top of Lafayette Avenue Extension in Hawthorne so I got up at three o'clock in the morning to give myself enough time to walk to Fifth Avenue in the Riverside Section of Paterson. The workers congregated on Fifth Avenue and marched to Market Street in East Paterson to the spot where Marcal Paper Company is now located.

We picketed that dye house until we were chased away by police. Carrying the American flag, our group of workers marched to the United Piece Dye Works on Fifth Avenue and picketed that shop. Our demonstration was a peaceful one, but the police came and threw tear gas bombs at us and hit us with their clubs.

Our union was Dyers Union Local 1733, United Textile Workers of America. Under the leadership of Anthony Amirato, President of the Dyers Local, the Local grew from 1,800 members in 1933 to 13,000 in January of 1935. We fought for the rights of the textile workers, rights people today take for granted.

—Arturo Mazzioti
November 16, 1906–December 29, 1998

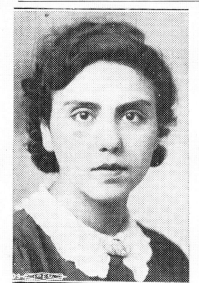

Born in Paterson to Italian immigrants in 1915, Marianna R. Fidone was 17 years old when she began at Arrow Piece Dye Works on 23rd Avenue. At age 18, she was elected assistant secretary-treasurer of Dyer's Local 1733 in 1933 and was elected secretary-treasurer in 1936, a post she held until 1952. She married Alfred Costa, a carpenter, and left the Dyer's Local 1733 to raise her family. She returned to work in 1962 as a clerk typist in Preakness Hospital, where she organized a union. Today, Marianna remains passionate about the philosophy of the Dyer's Local 1733. "My years with the 1733 shaped my life at a time when there was a cultural feeling that people should help each other, feelings which carried into the union itself as a whole," she recalls. "In 1933, we fought for a 40-hour work week, equal distribution of work on all shifts, a fair minimum wage, overtime, seniority protection, things that we fought for and won. We must continue to educate our children on our rights, not just to have the rich run things for you." (Courtesy Sol Stetin.)

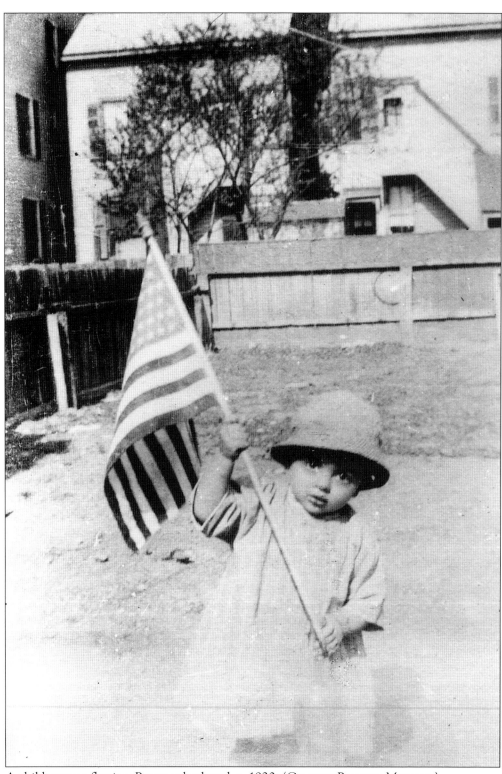
A child waves a flag in a Paterson backyard, *c.* 1920. (Courtesy Paterson Museum.)

Three
MAIN STREET OF YESTERYEAR

In the 1920s, Paterson, like many cities in the Northeast, defined itself in terms of the buoyant prosperity of the Jazz Age. During the Coolidge years, the standard of living had dramatically advanced and almost anything seemed possible. Paterson supported three daily newspapers and their pages were filled with community news and advertising. In 1923, *The Paterson Press Guardian* caught the temper of the times when it claimed that Paterson was a place "where genuine wholesome hospitality is formed within its gates—a real hometown for the people."

Paterson had an abundance of civic, fraternal, and sporting organizations. However, it was Main Street, particularly the area between Grand and Broadway, that acted as a magnet for residents and visitors. On any given weekday, the district bustled with activity. Shoppers flocked to Main Street's inviting retail establishments by auto and trolley for the "wholesome hospitality" the *Guardian* wrote about. It would be no exaggeration to characterize the Main Street of the 1920s as a shopper's Mecca.

During the first years of the 19th century, Main Street had a rustic, hamlet-like appearance. It was a dusty, sometimes muddy place, with the stillness broken by the sound of horses, wagons, and people on their way to banks, taverns, and other small businesses. Visitors included country farmers who had legal matters at the county seat. The Passaic Hotel, a noted establishment, welcomed those who desired liquid refreshment on hot summer days. By the 1870s, Paterson had attained its reputation for industrial eminence and farmers descended on the city late in the evening to sell their produce. They would load their wagons, and then wait on side streets off Main until midnight, when they could legally secure their favorite parking places for the following day's trade. Market days were Tuesdays, Thursdays, and Saturdays.

This homespun picture had changed dramatically by the 1920s. The booming "Silk City of America," with a population of 136,000, ranked as the state's third largest city, and contained some 20,000 dwellings, four department stores, and an estimated 3,000 retail establishments. Many Patersonians found employment in the city's silk mills. There was no longer evidence of the devastating February 1902 fire, which ravaged the central business district. As one journalist reported, the city had quickly reconstructed its "burned marts of trade."

A dwindling number of people today can recall the stores that once lined both sides of Main Street. There were businesses like the Van Dyk Furniture Company, with floor upon floor of select home furnishings. There was the Mart, a hive of activity that lured customers by boasting it was the "Miracle Store of New Jersey." Shopping in Paterson was incomplete without a stop at Quackenbush's, which offered quality goods for decades. In the later 1920s, the store was acquired by the Newark-based Hahne's and thus lost its independent status.

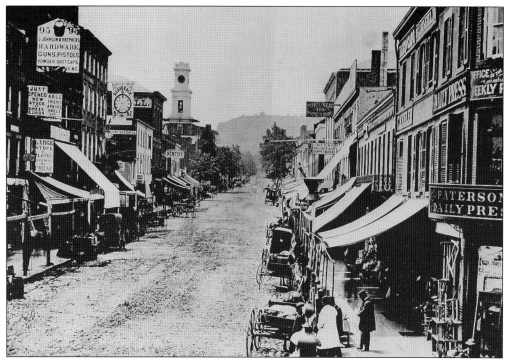
Horses and buggies dominate the streets in this 1868 southern view of Main Street looking toward Broadway. (Courtesy Paterson Museum.)

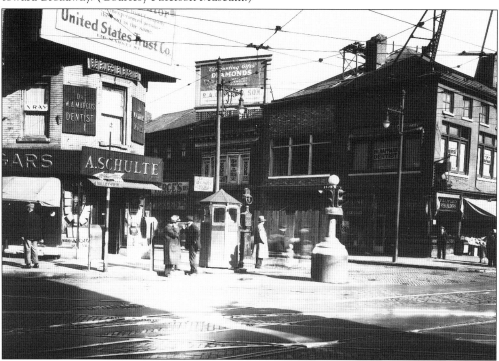
Trolley car rails prevailed on Broadway and Main Streets during the 1920s. (Courtesy Paterson Museum.)

But the department store that was synonymous with Paterson, a family-owned and managed store with legions of admirers, was Meyer Brothers. Located at 179 Main Street, the building occupied an entire city block. It had five floors, almost 80 departments, and, during the holiday season, it employed nearly 1,000 people.

The store had been an institution in Paterson since the 1880s. Aaron, David and Leopold Meyer, dry-goods merchants from Newark, believed Paterson would provide an excellent marketplace for their wares. The three brothers originally traded under the name of the "Boston Store." Customers could rely on finding a wide selection of goods at low prices. Business boomed and the brothers decided to purchase property on Washington Street, directly in back of the Main Street store. Eventually, the name Boston Store was dropped. When the Paterson Fire of 1902 gutted the original building, the store was rebuilt grander than ever. Elevators whisked customers from floor to floor, where they were greeted by tastefully arranged displays of carpets, furniture, clothing, dressmaking items, and a vast selection of other merchandise. Meyer Brothers told its patrons that clerks spoke "nearly every European language."

In time, Aaron Meyer purchased the interest of his two brothers and operated the store himself until April 13, 1925, when his son Bertram became proprietor. "Bert" Meyer, who never married, looked upon the store as an extension of his family. During his tenure, Meyer Brothers developed an unparalleled reputation for excellence in goods and services, which approached and exceeded the standards set by the larger Manhattan and Philadelphia department stores.

After assuming the reigns of management, Bert Meyer had the store completely redecorated. The woodwork was beautifully finished in solid and matched walnut veneers. Impeccably dressed, Meyer, who later resided in the Alexander Hamilton Hotel, routinely circulated through his retail domain, on the alert for imperfections in service and appearance. One employee had the task of caring for the woodwork, and he spent all of his time oiling and polishing what seemed like walls of walnut. The facade of the landmark store contained ornate bronze grillwork and this, too, Meyer routinely inspected, making certain it never allowed to dull. He invested his money in creating a classy showplace for downtown Paterson, and many of those who worked for him remained there for the rest of their working lives.

Charles Feitlowitz worked for the store nearly 50 years and retired as director of display. In a 1987 interview, he fondly remembered the store's Main Street entrance: "It was my favorite," he said, "because it had an arched ceiling done in 14-carat gold leaf, beautiful marble trim under the windows, artistic brass and bronze work in the vestibule, and a lovely ceiling fixture." Seymour Ackerman was another Meyer Brother's employee who Meyer developed and promoted to the store's benefit. Joining the store as an errand boy, Ackerman remained with Meyer Brothers for 44 consecutive years, retiring in 1954 as merchandising manager.

Meyer Brothers was famous for attracting customers from near and far to its seasonal sale events. At the Washington Street entrance, they were greeted by doorman Jack Demarest, appropriately outfitted in an impressive gold-braided navy uniform. Demarest assisted ladies with their packages as they waited for either their limousines or the store shuttle bus. The store's busy beauty shop attracted many well-to-do women, although many Paterson schoolteachers came to have their hair done as well. It was located on the store's balcony and was known as the "green room" after its resplendent tiles.

Bertram Meyer died in January 1963, leaving a flurry of bequests to loyal employees and $3 million to establish a charitable foundation in memory of his beloved parents. After more than a century in Paterson, the imposing building on Main Street closed its doors for good in 1987. It was a long and good run. Few stores could claim the affection Meyer Brothers had instilled in the hearts and memories of its generations of customers. Meyer Brothers was about loyalty—an unspoken bond that seems to have survived time itself as it still lives in those who remember Main Street during its golden era.

—Edward A. Smyk

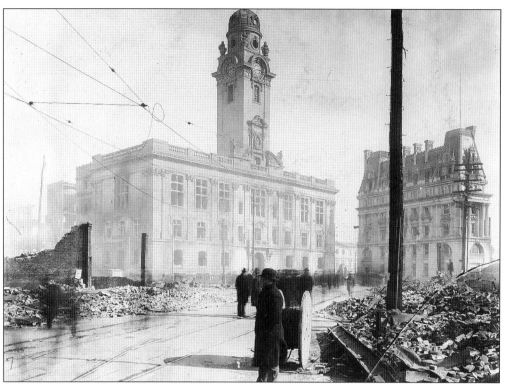

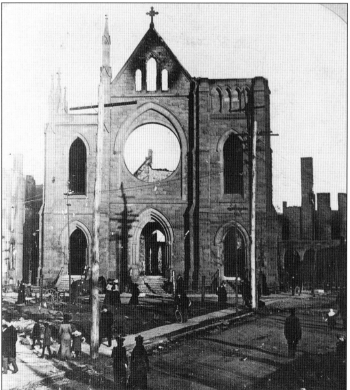

On the night of February 8, 1902, a fire began between Broadway and Van Houten Streets in a building used to house railway cars. The view above is of Paterson's City Hall amidst the destruction of the Market Street area; the photograph to the left is of the skeletal remains of St. Joseph's Roman Catholic Church and Rectory on the corner of Caroll and Market Streets. The devastating blaze killed one person, left hundreds of families homeless, and also destroyed police headquarters, three schools, a library, and 30 office buildings. (Photos courtesy Paterson Museum.)

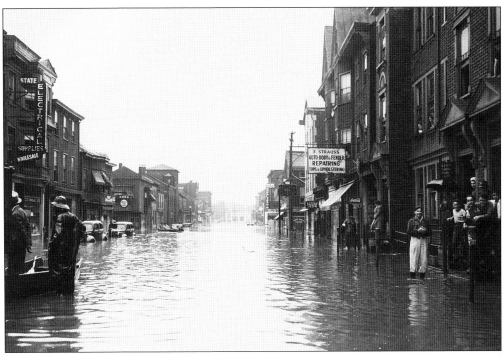

Only four weeks after the Great Fire of 1902, the Passaic River flooded, killing six people and destroying homes, businesses, and roads. The Army Engineers called the dual disaster "a once in a century coincidence." In October of 1903, another rainfall set off more destructive flooding. A major flood occurred in 1936, as depicted in these photographs. Flooding continues. A severe flood in April of 1984 caused damage estimated in the millions. (Photos courtesy Paterson Museum.)

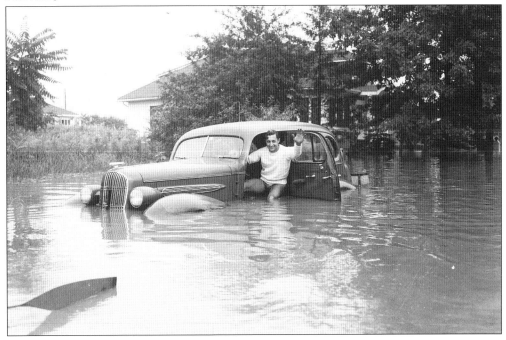

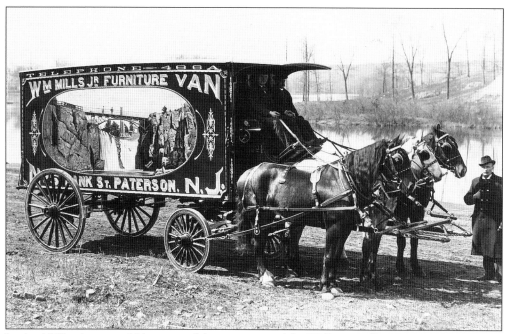

In the 1890s, this incredibly ornate delivery wagon of the William Mills Jr. Furniture Company featured a painting of the Great Falls. Truly an artful display of individualism at its retail finest! (Courtesy Passaic County Historical Society.)

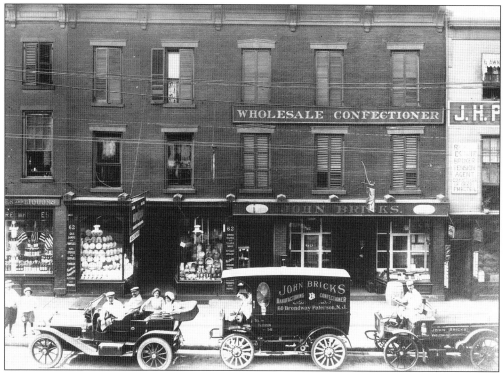

John Bricks Wholesale Confectioner was located on 60 Broadway, c. 1900. (Passaic County Historical Society.)

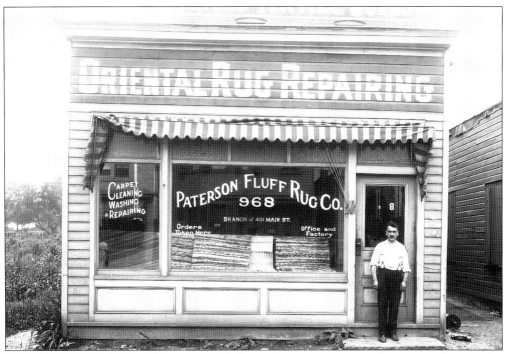
A worker stands in front of the Paterson Fluff Rug Company, an oriental rug repair shop, in this c. 1910 photo. (Courtesy Paterson Museum.)

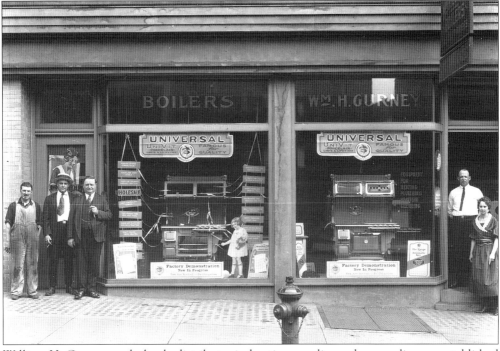
William H. Gurney, a wholesale distributor in heating supplies and gas appliances, established his successful business in 1912 at 181–185 Ellison Street. Today, the area is a parking lot for Passaic County Community College. (Courtesy Paterson Museum.)

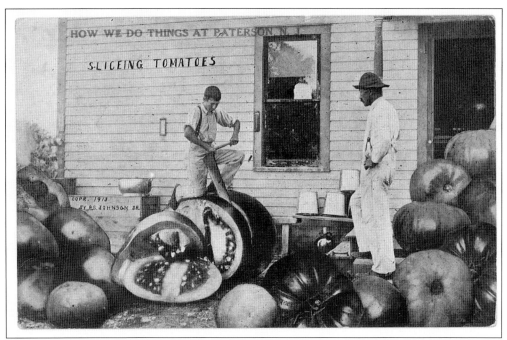

The c. 1913 novelty postcards on this and the following page are titled "How We Do Things At Paterson, NJ." Pride in Silk City is clearly, albeit absurdly, illustrated in these postcards, which feature Jersey tomatoes so big they need to be sliced with a saw, apples imposing enough to keep any doctor away, and gargantuan fish that simply do not get away. (All three courtesy Paterson Museum.)

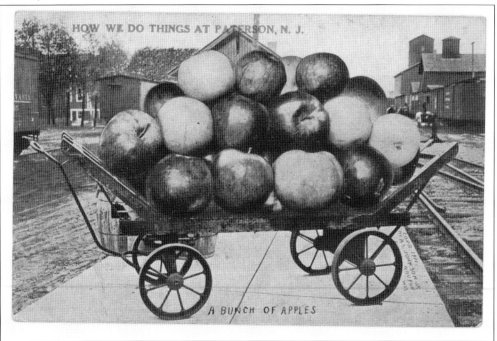

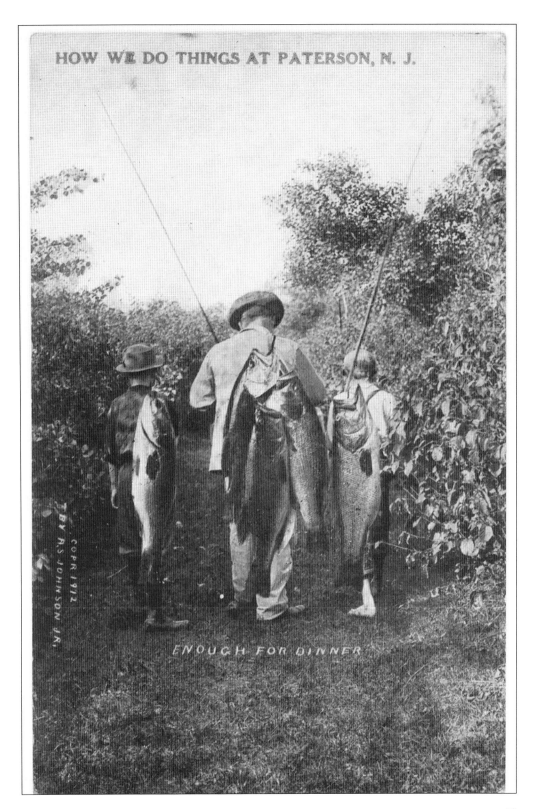

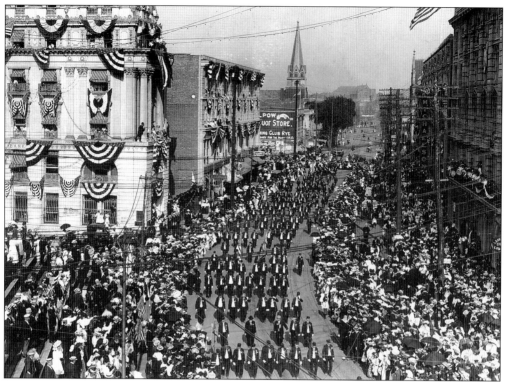

Thousands gathered on Market Street for this WWI Armistice parade. Below are patriotic parade participants from the Loyal Order of Moose. (Courtesy Paterson Museum.)

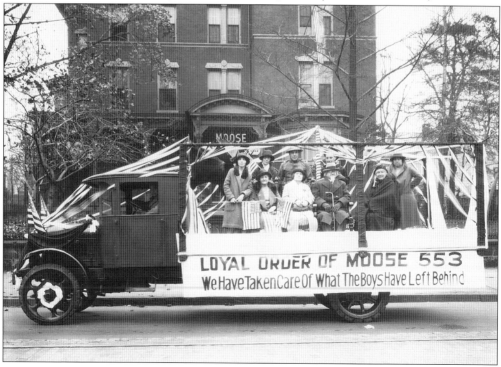

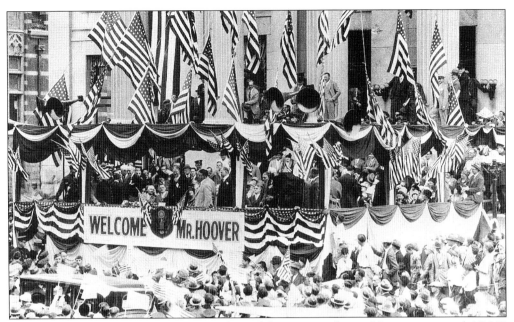

Herbert Hoover, Republican presidential candidate, was welcomed by an estimated 15,000 people at the Passaic County courthouse during his election campaign on September 18, 1928. Herman Robert Leonhard, a Columbia University student at the time, took this photo of the platform erected for the event. (Courtesy Edward A. Smyk.)

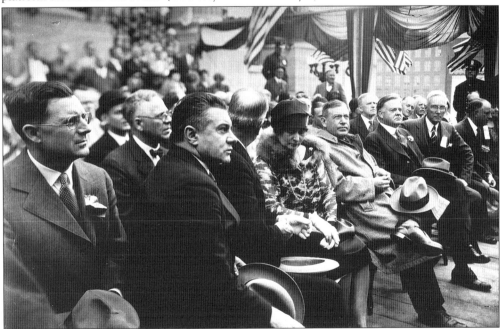

Hoover awaits his introduction. Shown here are, from left to right, George M. Mitchell, candidate for mayor; Hamilton Fish Kean (head turned), candidate for U.S. Senate; Elsa H. Flower, Republican state committeewoman; U.S. Senator Walter E. Edge; Herbert Hoover; Rep. George N. Seger; and Morgan F. Larson, gubernatorial candidate. (Courtesy Edward A. Smyk, *Paterson Evening News* photograph.)

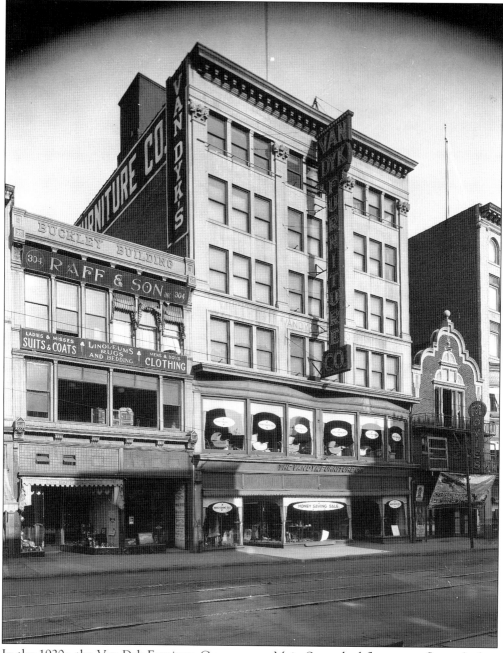
In the 1920s, the Van Dyk Furniture Company on Main Street had floor upon floor of select home furnishings. It is now a bargain store called El Mundo. (Courtesy Paterson Museum.)

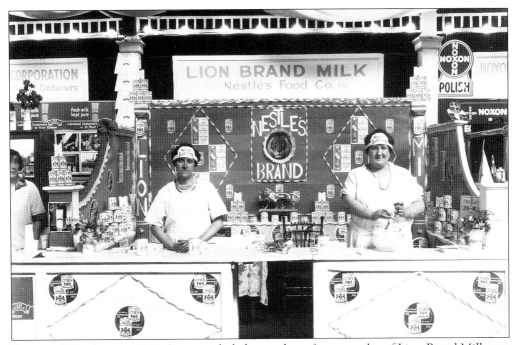

Early retail displays on Main Street included everything from samples of Lion Brand Milk to a patriotic tribute to Potato Week in Paterson. (Photos courtesy Paterson Museum.)

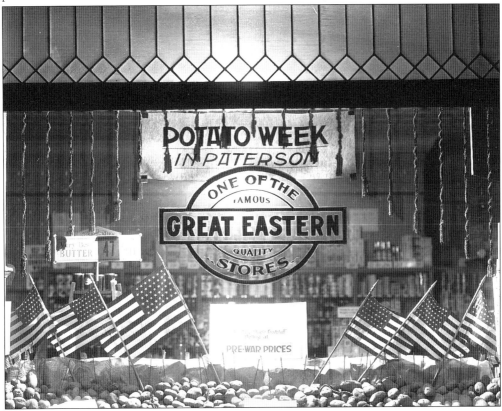

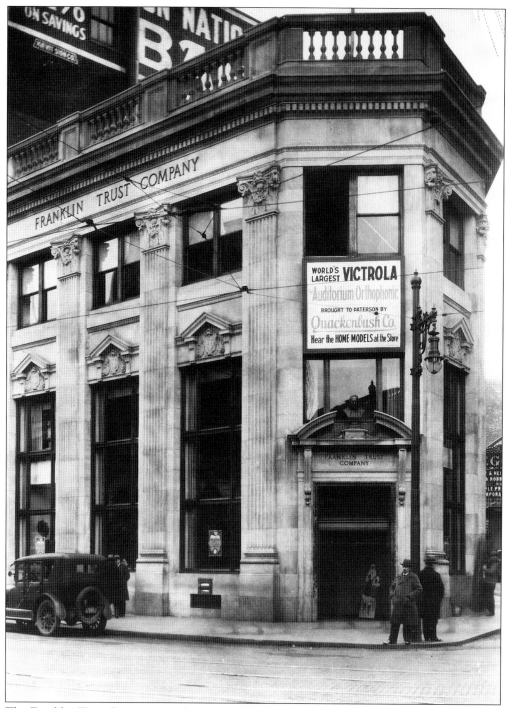

The Franklin Trust Company was located on Market Street across from Paterson City Hall. In this 1920s photograph, there is a Victrola advertisement for Quackenbush Company. Chase Bank now occupies the building. (Courtesy Paterson Museum.)

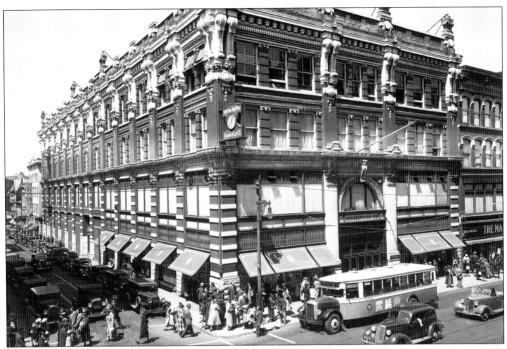

The Quackenbush Company is shown here in all its grandeur as it existed in the 1930s. Next door, there was the Mart, a hive of activity that lured customers by boasting it was the "Miracle Store of New Jersey." Today, the beautiful architecture of Quackenbush is covered over with a plastic facade, the fate of many buildings in downtown Paterson. National Wholesale Liquidators is now located at the former Quackenbush location. (Courtesy Paterson Museum.)

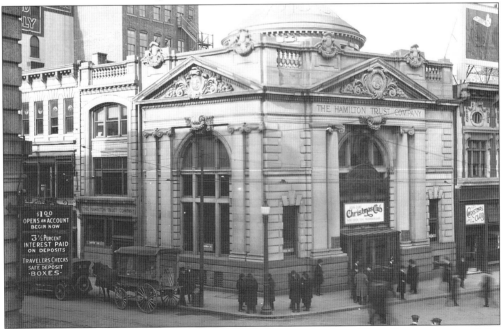

At the turn of the century, the Hamilton Trust Company bank on Main Street was one of the city's most elegant buildings. (Courtesy Paterson Museum.)

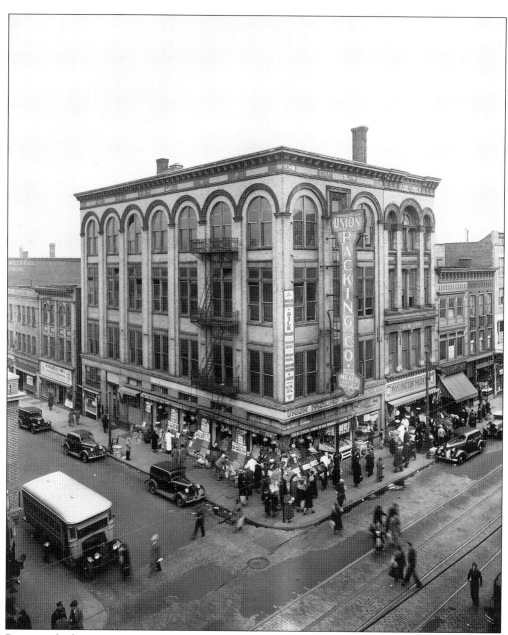

Paterson had numerous newspapers at one time, including the *Morning Call*, the city's first morning daily, established on October 1, 1885, by Edward B. Haines. In 1889, Haines sold the newspaper to the Call Printing and Publishing Company, a corporation with a board composed of 47 "prominent and responsible Republican citizens." The *Morning Call* was bought out again by the *Bergen Evening Record* in 1969 and was then sold to the News Printing and Publishing Company when it merged with the *Paterson Evening News*. In this 1935 photograph, the old Morning Call building, located at 83 Broadway, can be seen to the right of the Union Packing Company. (Courtesy Paterson Museum.)

The *Paterson Evening News*, an afternoon daily, was also established by Edward B. Haines on December 22, 1890. His son, Harry B. Haines, assumed control of the *News* in 1911 when the paper had three daily competitors: the *Paterson Daily Press*, the *Paterson Daily Guardian*, and the *Morning Call*. Dubbed "Paterson's Foremost Newspaper," the *News* was originally located on Ellison Street before moving its headquarters in 1962 to "News Plaza" on Straight Street. That facility closed in 1986 when the *News* merged with the *Herald News* in Passaic. Paterson has lacked a daily newspaper to call its own since. The *Record*, based in the nearby suburb of Wayne, bought the *North Jersey Herald & News* in 1998. (Courtesy Paterson Museum.)

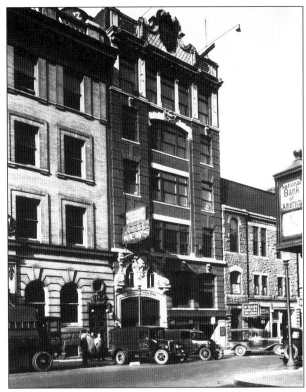

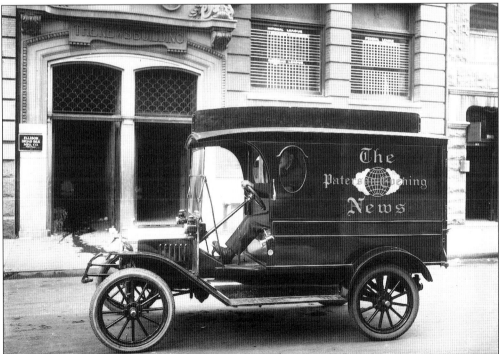

This delivery truck was for the *Paterson Evening News* on Ellison Street, c. 1920. (Courtesy Paterson Museum.)

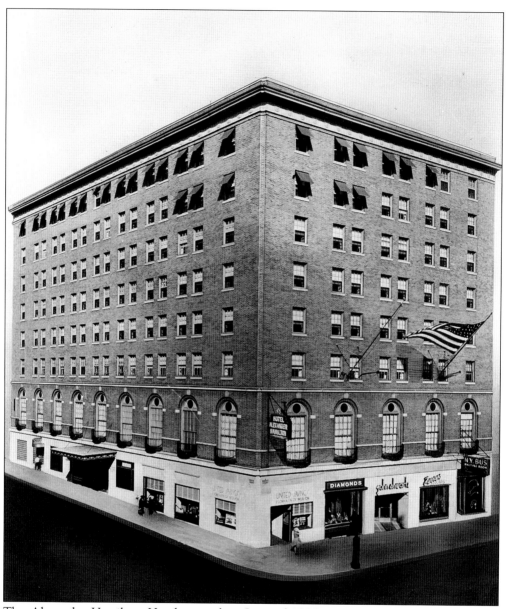

The Alexander Hamilton Hotel opened in June of 1925. Designed by Paterson architect Frederick W. Wentworth, the 210-room colonial-style building featured a luxurious ballroom with crystal chandeliers, murals depicting the history of the silk industry, an assembly room with silk wall coverings in gold and lavender, and an elegant dining area. Today, the Alexander Hamilton is a welfare hotel for the homeless. (Courtesy Paterson Museum.)

Bertram Meyer (1884–1963) assumed management of Meyer Brothers, the family department store, on April 13, 1925, and operated it until his death. This photo was taken at Atlantic City, his favorite resort. On September 26, 1933, Meyer inscribed this photo to H.B. Haines (1882–1972) publisher of the *Paterson Evening News*. The inscription reads: "To HBH, My very best friend." (Graf Archives, Courtesy Edward A. Smyk.)

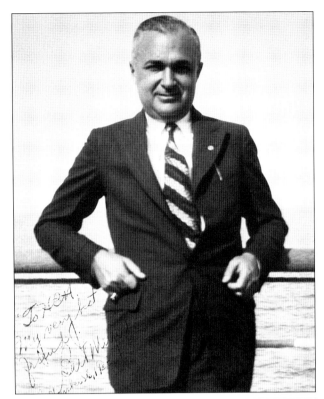

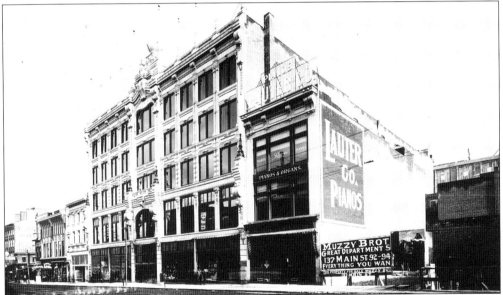

This 1903 photograph of the Meyer Brothers Department Store shows some of the damage caused by the Great Fire of 1902. The store was completely destroyed by fire in 1991. Only one ornate stone pillar of the legendary establishment remains today, on which a plaque was dedicated in memory of John Anthony Nicosia, a 29-year-old firefighter with Company No. 4 who died battling the downtown blaze. A new "mall type" structure has since replaced the store. (Courtesy Paterson Museum.)

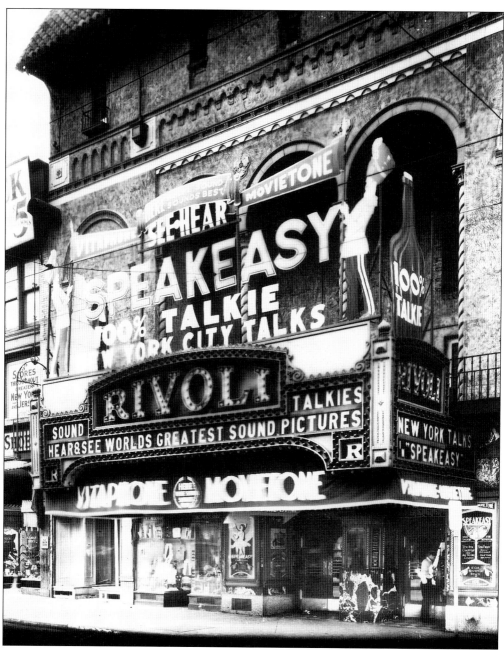

Paterson was once viewed as a first-rate theatrical center that earned the popular saying: "If the production goes well in Paterson, it can go anywhere." Dozens of theaters thrived, drawing people from miles away to the heart of Paterson. Not a single theater remains open today. The enchanting Rivoli Theater, built in 1923 at 130 Main Street, is shown here. (Courtesy Paterson Museum.)

Four

AT THE MOVIES

In the 1950s, the downtown movie houses in Paterson were a regular feature of life, especially on Saturdays. They were filled with people of all ages, but mostly the young who went there to watch the genre features—horror, comedy, and science fiction—roll across the screen several times each afternoon. At that time my friends and I were relatively young (all under 10 years old), but we never went to the movies with our parents. Families went to the drive-ins, an early indication of the encroachment of the automobile.

However, we were free, in ways that many children today are no longer free (unless you count meaningless consumer "choice" as a part of freedom), and so we found our way, almost always on foot, winding toward the downtown through the micro-neighborhoods between our homes and the beating heart of the city. A small knot of mainly white kids, we traversed the domains of the Syrian, black, and Puerto Rican communities that opened up along our path and then closed after us, each at a different stage of development and expression, each a tentative opening into the Paterson of today.

My friends and I never read a newspaper to find out what was playing, nor did we plan or otherwise map out our voyages to the downtown theaters. Today there is not a single movie house left in Paterson, a stark reality given the 10-plex movie palaces that flourish along the highways. Back then, we simply went walking down Marshall or Main or Straight Streets, veering off the main route here and there to establish a detour, but always winding up in the same place, because Paterson is a small city, dense with vagaries but still distinguishable as an intimate and, I think, profoundly knowable place.

We knew the neighborhood kids, the neighborhood dogs, and the neighborhood streets. We knew where and how the distinct spaces blended into and out of one another and what that meant in a rudimentary, street-smart sort of way. Had we lived further from the urban core our experience might have been different, but we were privileged to live close to the center, and could thus range inward as well as outward, toward the peripheries. As a result we came to know and appreciate the city.

Since leaving, I've returned to Paterson regularly, first to visit my grandmother, who had resisted the suburban impulse, then to go to college, and more recently to do the work that I do as folklorist, ethnohistorian, and ethnographer.

On one such occasion in 1994, I went to Garret Mountain to walk around for a while, and afterwards sat down on a bench beside a sloping grassy field with woods on three sides and a vista of sorts on the fourth, looking vaguely toward Rifle Camp Road and the Great Notch in the mountains beyond. This was a deeply familiar place and I soon began to relish the sensation of my experience there in two distinct time periods, then and now.

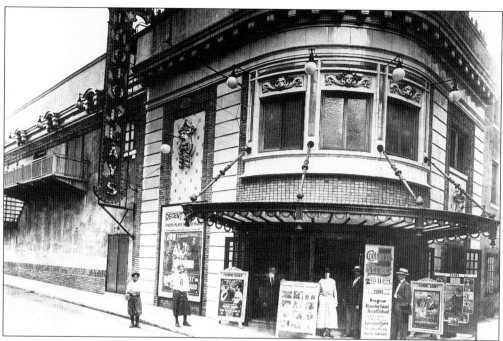

Built by movie pioneer Jacob Fabian, the Regent Theater became the first moving picture theater in Passaic County when it opened on September 14, 1914, on Union and Smith Streets. On opening night the crowd was so great the police had to be called. Moving picture skeptics called the theater "Fabian's Folly," but were soon proved wrong. The Regent featured a movie along with the live theatrical entertainment of talents like Bob Hope, Molley Goldberg, Morton Downey, Milton Berle, and Duke Ellington and his band. The site is now a parking lot. (Courtesy Paterson Museum.)

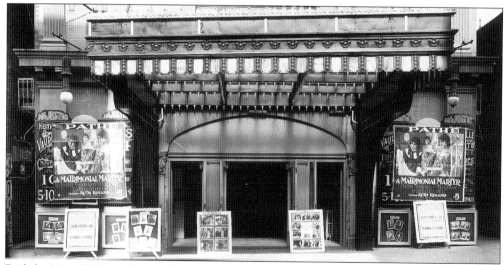

Built by Max Gold in 1910 at 293 Main Street, the Majestic Theater featured the best in live vaudeville talent, with names like Abbott and Costello, Red Skelton, Hank Ladd, Edith Fellows, and Virginia Mayo. In 1926, the theater's policy switched to movies, but live vaudeville acts continued until 1952, a remarkable run. The movie *A Matrimonial Martyr* was featured when this photograph was taken. (Courtesy Paterson Museum.)

The sky was open and bright, and the city lay quietly nearby beneath the lookout point above Marshall Street. I, too, sat quietly, a feeling of deep harmony overtaking me, but soon there was a distraction in the trees to my left when three young people, Peruvians—two older, one very small—emerged. A soccer ball was clamped under an arm, but the ball rolled out onto the grass and the boys arrayed themselves into positions for an ad hoc game. They played, feinting and kicking, age differences dissolving into the common movement, sky and field merging to encompass it all—their voices, their busy legs, the sound of the ball brushing through the grass, the birdsong drifting from nearby trees, the sun an almost audible presence in the heightened air. In the sheer openness of that moment, the cosmic whole was suddenly, playfully revealed.

Gradually, others entered the scene from the same patch of woods, carrying bags and a blanket. There were women and men, an infant, and young girls, and they spread themselves and their things into the grass space just above the game. And the game grew, billowing into this developing context, and the soccer boys, playing hard, laughed and murmured among themselves. The women reached into their bags and began passing food around—tamales, corn on the cob, meat on the bone. The people ate, some breaking away momentarily from the game, one by one, to obtain bits of the food, then chewing and playing, legs marking the action, and all the while their laughter, their playful voices spiraled through the orchestrated, mindful movements of the now living ball and filled the air, bursting with optimism and the teeming possibilities of life and of hope. All the while the city, my city and theirs, lay just beyond and outside it all, a bundle of temporalities tied with a *taja*.

Later, memory supplied a reference: the opening scenes of an Antonioni movie, because in the blazing sunlight the event had appeared so cinematic, so much like a dream or an oversized reality. In fact, a conjunction had occurred then and, with it, the realization that the lives of those Peruvians—migrants in the 1990s—were broadly akin to my own life in the 1950s as a grandson of migrants. Both sets of lives, commingling now in my memory, were discovering forms of freedom while coping with daunting and difficult conditions. Knowing this, what else can free people do but act freely against prejudice, against nostalgia, against the would-be monocultures of the non-urban spaces? Or they can make provision for tolerance, for hope, and for the full and ongoing range of human and earthly possibility, in the city and elsewhere, then and now, speaking with our many-colored tongues.

—Tom Carroll DeBlasio

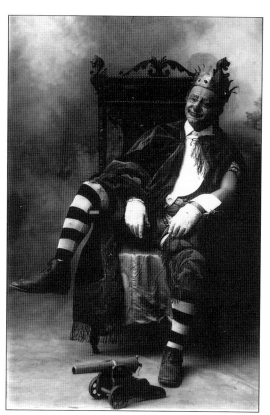

An unidentified Paterson vaudeville clown poses for a photographer. (Courtesy Paterson Museum.)

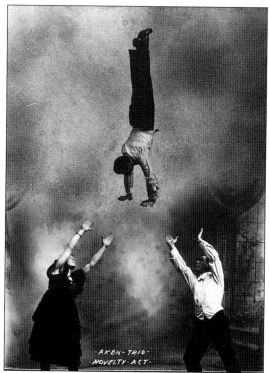

The Aken Trio was one of many acts to perform live in Paterson's theaters. (Courtesy Paterson Museum.)

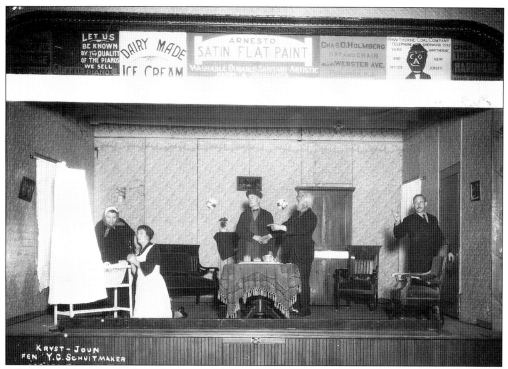

All the world was indeed on the stages of Paterson, from burlesque comedy and novelty acts to tear-jerker tragedies and lavish stage spectaculars. (Photos courtesy Paterson Museum.)

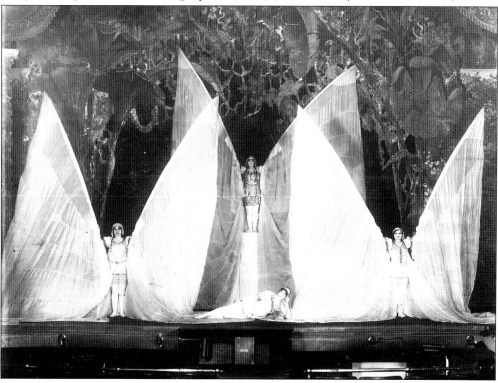

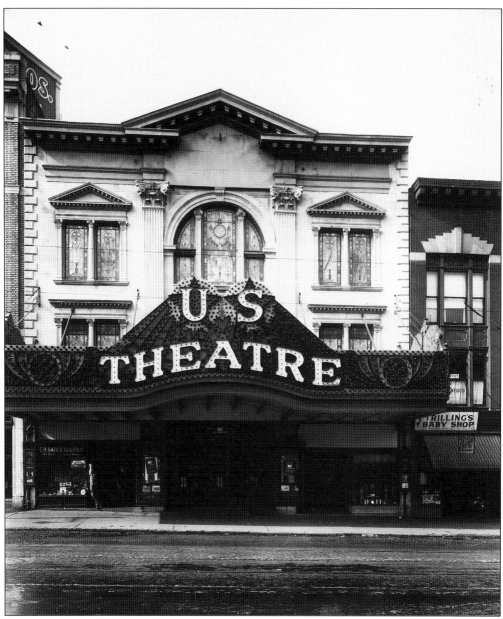
The U.S. Theater was opened by the Adams brothers at 284 Main Street in 1916 on the site of the Old Walden's Opera House, which had been constructed in 1866. In later years, the vaudeville theater featured such classic films as *It Happened One Night* and *For Whom the Bell Tolls*. (Courtesy Paterson Museum.)

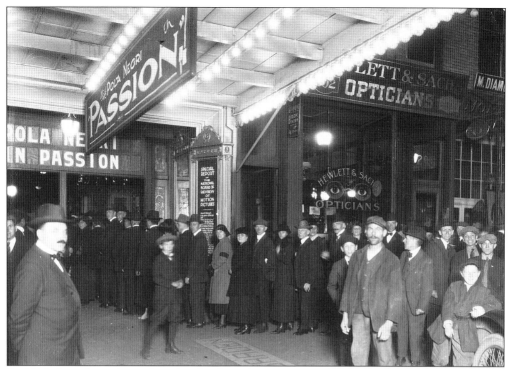

In 1919, long lines formed at the Garden Theater on Market Street to see *Passion* starring Pola Negri. Built in 1915, the theater was knocked down to clear space for Hamilton Plaza. (Courtesy Paterson Museum.)

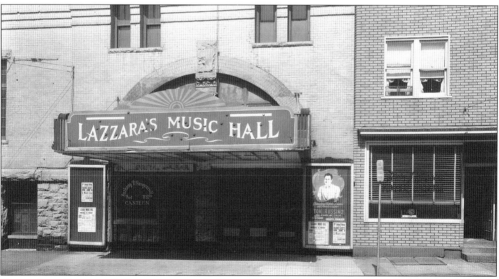

Formerly a Swiss and German music hall on Cross Street (now Cianci Street) in the early 1900s, Cosmo Lazzara opened Lazzara's Music Hall in the 1930s. Lazzara's featured a dance hall, live Italian "soap opera" stage plays, boxing, wrestling, and noted Italian singers, like Carlo Buti. The site is now a parking lot. Lazzara was also known for his successful bakery on Cross Street, later renamed Cianci Street after Msgr. Carlo Cianci, who became pastor of St. Michael's R.C. Church in 1919. (Courtesy Paterson Museum.)

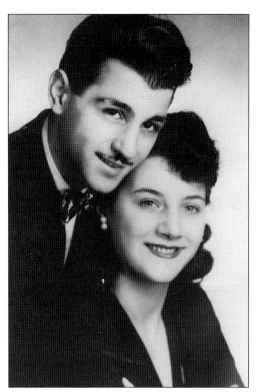

Like many Patersonians, Muriel Zofrea and her husband, Dominic "Butchie" Zofrea, loved the downtown theaters. "My Butchie's favorite was the Majestic," says Muriel, who lived on Passaic Street in the 1940s and now resides in senior housing on Passaic and Ellison Streets. "Me, I'd sneak in the Orpheum and sit with the men to watch all the stage girls bounce around, and later I loved auction night at the State Theater when I'd fill my purse with hard boiled eggs, screwdrivers, everything, so if they called out that item you'd get a prize. Forget about it! Those were the days." Here, Muriel and Butchie, who passed away in 1994, pose at Leo's Studio on Market Street in 1946. (Courtesy Muriel Zofrea.)

The Orpheum Theater on Van Houten Street opened in 1921 featuring the 150-pound-plus "Beef Trust" beauties and live comedy acts, like Abbott and Costello. Mae West made a brief appearance at the burlesque house, but she was reportedly carried away in a paddy wagon one night because of her risqué routine. The Orpheum later became the State Theater with 1,400 seats. Like a faded tattoo, the words "Classy and Refined Burlesque" can still barely be read on the side of the vacant building, now owned by the Islamic Foundation of New Jersey. (Courtesy Tom Ufer.)

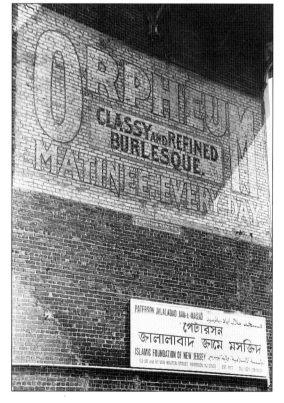

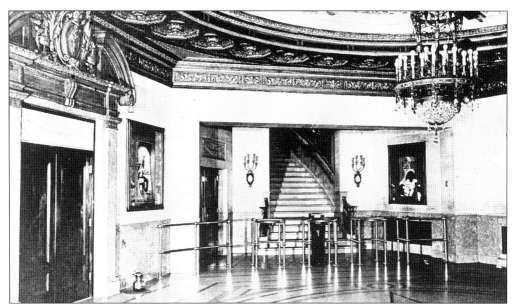

Above: The lobby of the Fabian Theater, located on Church Street, was photographed *c.* 1925. Known previously for its artistic murals, two-ton chandelier, marble balustrades, and ornate guilding, in 1992 the Fabian became the last Paterson theater to close, when the deteriorating neighborhood deterred patrons. Ironically, Jacob Fabian decided to build his show palace when he heard about the elegant plans on the adjacent corner for the Alexander Hamilton Hotel. Opening night on December 14, 1925, featured the movie *We Moderns* and classical music from the Fabian Grand Orchestra. In its final days, the five-screen theater showed kill flicks like *Freddy's Dead* and *Body Parts*. A Fabian executive said at the time of the closing: "Nobody wants to come there to operate a theater and no one wants to come down there and watch a movie." (Courtesy of Edward A. Smyk.) *Below:* The once bustling ticket booth still stands, with a "We Buy Gold" sign left from a defunct business. (Courtesy Ellen Denuto.)

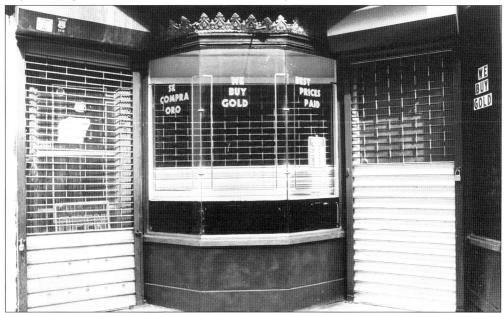

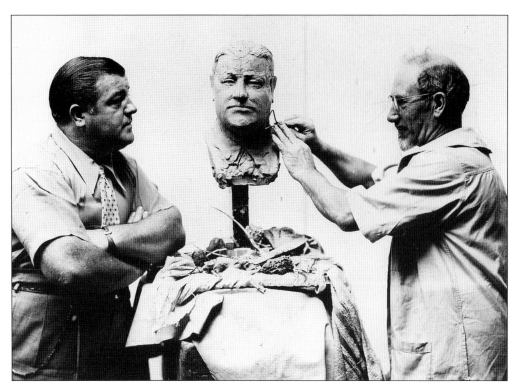

Prolific sculptor Gaetano Federici (1880–1964) puts the final touches on his bust of famed "Baa-a-aad Boy" comedian Lou Costello (1906–1959) during a 1942 meeting in Paterson. Born Louis Francis Cristillo on Madison Street, Costello managed to slip in plugs about his hometown in his movies every chance he could. As a boy, he frequented Paterson's vaudeville and movie theaters, where he first saw his idol, Charlie Chaplin. Lou's father, a weaver, wanted his son to be a doctor, but the clown later said he was way too busy at Public School 15 hiding his classmates coats and hats, sneaking frogs into class, and writing "I'm a bad boy" hundreds of times on the chalkboard after school. In later years, the die-hard Patersonian made sure his films, like *One Night in the Tropics* (1940), made their premieres at the Fabian Theater. Federici, one of eight children born to Italian immigrants, grew up in Paterson, where many of the sculptures from his Market Street studio still grace the city's streets, public buildings, churches, and graveyards. "Without my studio, I am like a turtle without its shell," said Federici in 1960. (Courtesy Paterson Museum.)

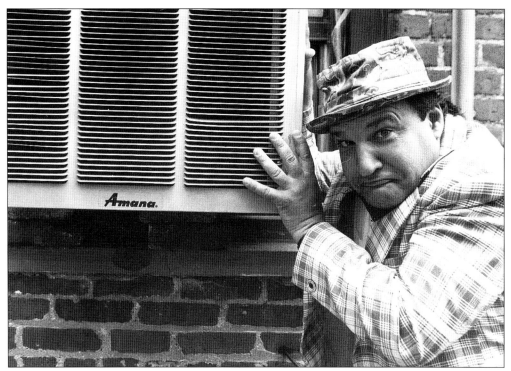

First-rate vaudeville lives on in the revealing parodies of Paterson native Floyd Vivino, star of the long-running *Uncle Floyd Show*. The television and nightclub clown is shown here expounding upon his hypothesis of how more than anything the Almighty Air-Conditioner changed urban America at a crucial time in history. In the old days, the theory goes, city folks would hang out on their front stoops, then they went inside to keep cool and just watch the boobtube. "Growing up in my old neighborhood on Sherman Avenue men might be playing cards on hot nights at Cesare Battisti's or Joe Vocatura a shoemaker who had a club," recalls Uncle Floyd. "One guy outside might say, 'Hey kid, here's a quarter, go get a soda or a lemon ice, bring me back one.' " Then, in the 1960s, came those chilling ads in papers like the *Paterson News* with the big letters AIR-CONDITIONING, dripping with cartoon icicles and the movie's name underneath it in small letters. "The movie wasn't the thing anymore, staying inside, off the streets, that's what mattered," says this Plato of Polyester, "More people these days are watching the world, not living it, knowing it." So there, you have it folks: *Air-conditioning and Isolation*. Perfect together? (By Jennifer Brown, Courtesy *North Jersey Herald & News*.)

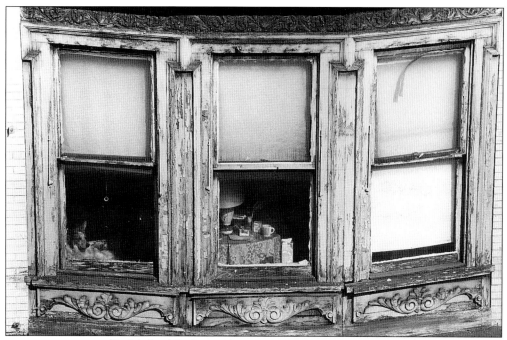

(By Michael R. Spozarsky, Courtesy Paterson Museum.)

Plaster saints, glass jewels
and those apt paper flowers, bafflingly
complex—have here
there forthright beauty, beside…

—William Carlos Williams, from *Paterson*.
Copyright 1946, 1948, 1951 by William Carlos Williams.
Reprinted by permission of New Directions Publishing Corp., NY.

Five

IN PATERSON

In memory of Tom Greco

On the corner of Market and Main
under the giant shadow of the Broadway Bank
gazing into shop windows, I feel like
one of those sixteenth century Dutch characters
lost in a crowd of local merchants
in one of Breughel's great paintings.
I wonder if there's a connection to anything
as I stand here with a head full of questions
like who put me in this picture,
when I should probably be off fishing somewhere
or finding my own place among the clouds
in another river-town surrounded by hills and factories.
Questions spill out of my head
like the twin rivers of my desire,
one happy, one sad to be alone.
And I know that there's a meaning to all this
now that you're gone
even the buildings look tired
And the streets a little sadder
even as I blend into this background
of weirdos and strangers
who stick their necks out like gargoyles
and shout obscenities from street corners

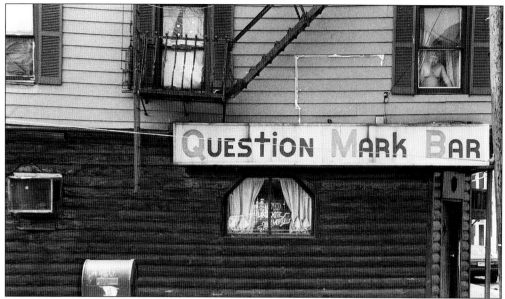

The Question Mark Bar, formerly the Nag's Head Tavern, was established in 1822 on Van Houten Street, in the heart of what has since been dubbed the Historic District. Giovanni Greco, owner of the Nag's Head and a silk worker, invited strikers and labor leaders from the IWW to use his bar as a meeting ground during the 1913 strike. His son Tommy recalled serving the strikers beer and soup for 5¢ as a young boy. (Courtesy Tom Ufer.)

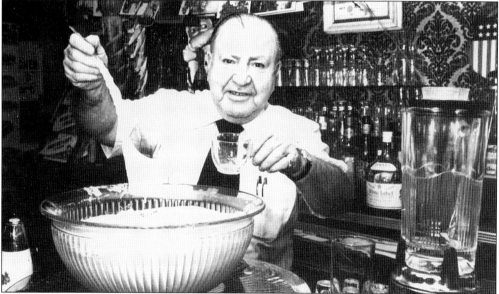

In this January 1, 1985 *Paterson News* photograph, bartender Tommy Greco serves up his "secret recipe"—Yuletide eggnog. A beloved friend to area patrons from all walks of life, Tommy was known as a class-act who loved his job. "They'll have to carry him out of this place," joked patrons. Indeed, Tommy died there in 1986. Now owned by Raymond Sotomayer, a native of Puerto Rico, the Question Mark remains a friendly local watering hole, one of the few bars downtown that has not succumbed to the monetary temptations of featuring go-go dancing. (Courtesy Paterson Museum.)

even as I watch a man dressed for winter
in the middle of July
dance to his own music
in the reflection of Jacob's Department Store.
Even as I enter Woolworth's
to buy something that will end up as garbage,
while others go around erecting huge monuments
to their failures.
And out of all this decay and poverty,
I see a Hispanic father bend down
to hug and kiss his son
in the squalor of Grand Street,
knowing we all begin and end
pretty much in the same way,
and the difference a little love
makes in our lives,
when I think of you
sitting in your chair by the window
and the sunlight you slept in,
or when you stood behind the bar
and gave us some comfort for our troubles,
when all we talked about
was the boredom around us,
and the jobs we hated,
and the places we call home.

—Mark Hillringhouse

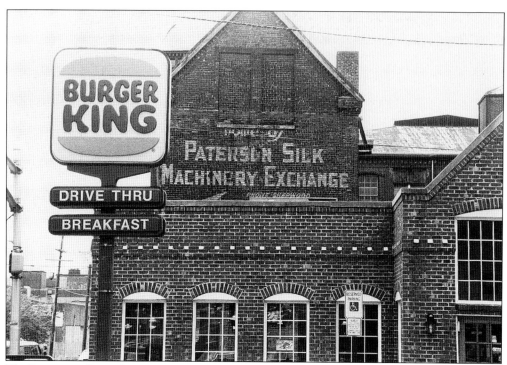
The Paterson Silk Machinery Exchange on Spruce Street was located in the former administrative offices (built in 1881) of the Rogers Locomotive Works. (Courtesy Tom Ufer.)

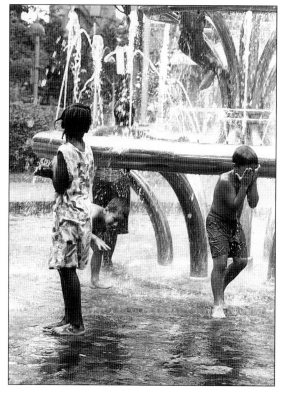
Children play at the fountain in Federici Park on nearby Cianci Street. (Courtesy Ellen Denuto.)

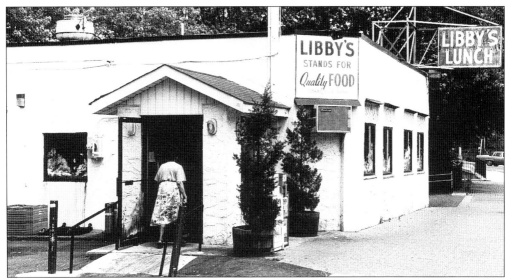

Established as "Pappas Lunch" by William Pappas in 1936, Libby's Lunch has been a Paterson institution on McBride Avenue ever since. Bought by Nick and Heidi Psarros in 1981, Libby's continues to be known for miles around for its "all the way" Texas wieners with special sauce and other Jersey diner fare. On some nights their daughter Voula serves up their specialities. Under the management of their son George, the family recently opened the Garden Cafe across the street, formerly the Olympic Diner, where cappuccinos and an array of desserts can be enjoyed in an outside seating area facing the Passaic River. (Courtesy Tom Ufer.)

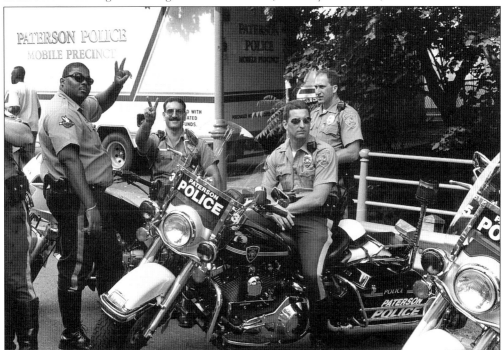

These Paterson motorcycle cops on Spruce Street are, from left to right, officers Gary Kersey, Mario Cercone, James Carrone, and Tommy Johnson. There are 405 police officers in the city. (Courtesy Giacomo De Stefano.)

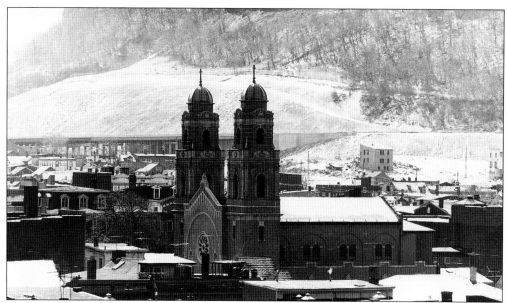

The downtown area was once dominated by large numbers of Scottish, Jewish, Irish, and German residents. Designed by Giuseppe Bellomo of Paterson, St. Michael's R.C. Church was built in 1928 to accommodate the growing population of Italian immigrants in the downtown area who were not welcomed at Saint John's Cathedral in Paterson. Formerly the sight of a small Methodist church built in 1836, the Roman Catholic Church bought the structure in 1903. Today, the neighborhood is ethnically mixed, mostly Hispanic. (By Michael R. Spozarsky, Courtesy Paterson Museum.)

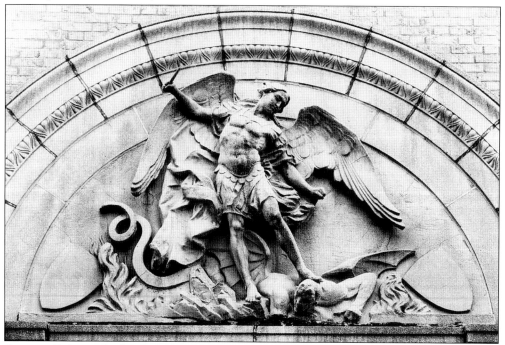

Gaetano Federici's high relief of cast stone depicts St. Michael overpowering Lucifer over the doors of St. Michael's R.C. Church. It was dedicated in 1928. (Courtesy Tom Ufer.)

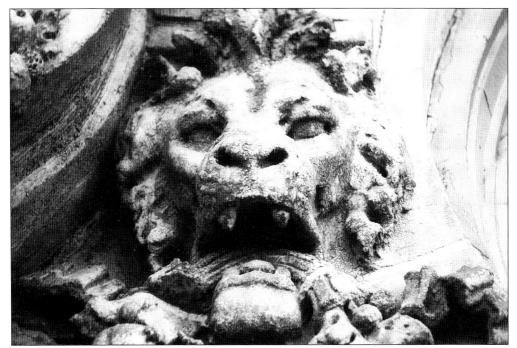

One only needs to look up to the heavens to see the beautiful details that still grace the unscathed portions of downtown architecture. This lion's head is one such celestial detail from a building on the corner of Washington and Ellison Streets built in 1902. There are no local laws mandating the protection of the physical facades of the downtown business area. (Courtesy Mark Hillringhouse.)

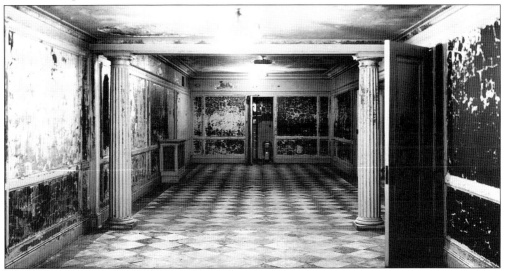

This photograph, entitled the "Masonic John," was taken in 1993 at the Masonic Temple on Broadway. To accommodate the ritualistic meetings of the abundant lodges in the Paterson area, the temple was built in 1923 "wherein principles might be inculcated, free from interruption by cowans and eavesdroppers." After falling into bankruptcy in the 1970s, the building fell into disrepair. Today, it is owned by the Jehovah Witnesses. (Courtesy Giacomo De Stefano.)

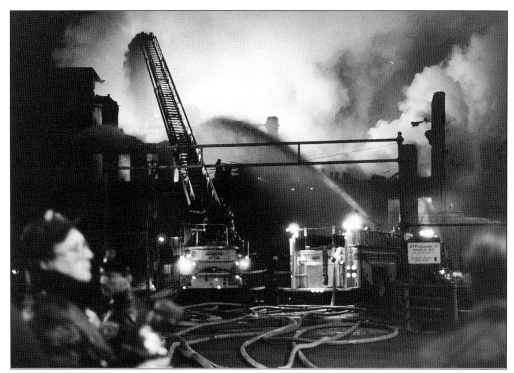

Despite the "Renaissance" plans spilled forth by a private developer group who bought many of the Historic District's buildings in 1983, a series of fires have since ravaged the Allied Textile Printing (ATP) complex on Van Houten Street, the site of various historic mills and manufacturing plants. The City of Paterson took ownership of the 7-acre site from the developer by tax foreclosure in 1993. By then, the city had lost a $1.6 million Urban Development Action Grant (UDAG) from the Department of Urban Affairs awarded upon financial and project status conditions. Since the 1980s, there have been an estimated 35 fires on the property, 12 of which were major blazes. Above, a four-alarm fire blazes away at the ATP site in 1989. (Courtesy Ellen Denuto.)

The last working factory on the ATP site was razed in 1983 and only a few factory facades, such as the front of the Waverly Mill (c. 1857) and part of the Colt Gun Factory (c. 1836), remain. Many homeless people now live in the ruins. Recent plans by Regan Development Corporation to buy the property from the city to develop townhouses have fallen under attack. Some area residents and their political allies have claimed that the site, located along the Passaic River, is an overlooked "scenic tourist opportunity," the development of which should be analyzed more closely. Others contend that historic concern for the site is past due. (Courtesy Ellen Denuto.)

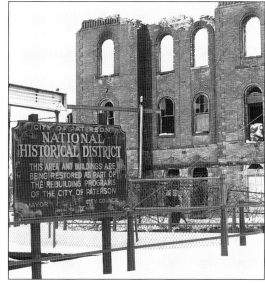

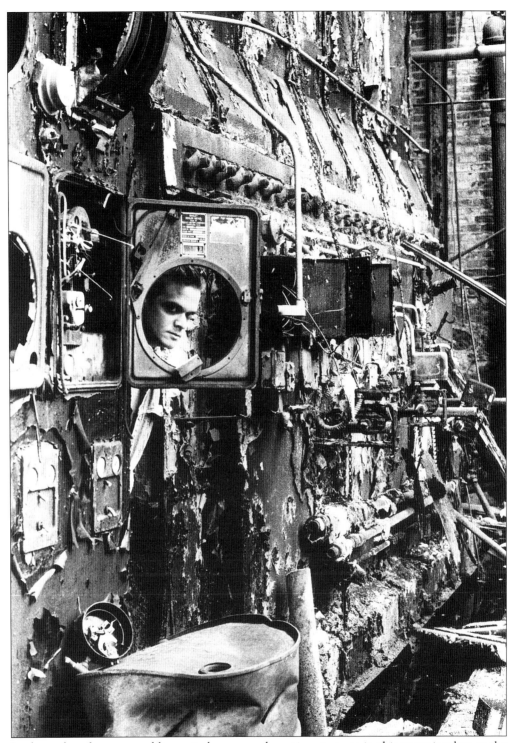
In the realm of art, a crumbling ruin becomes a haunting stage, as in this portrait taken at the ATP site by Tom Ufer of Tom Lanier, both residents of nearby artist housing, the Essex and Phoenix Mills. (Courtesy Tom Ufer.)

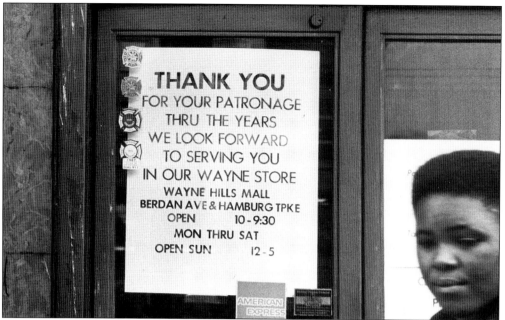

Established in the 1880s, Meyer Brothers was the elegant retail store that became most synonymous with downtown Paterson. The establishment closed its doors at 179 Main Street on March 15, 1987. The Wayne branch eventually closed as well. (Courtesy Joseph Pascalli, *The Mill Street Forward*.)

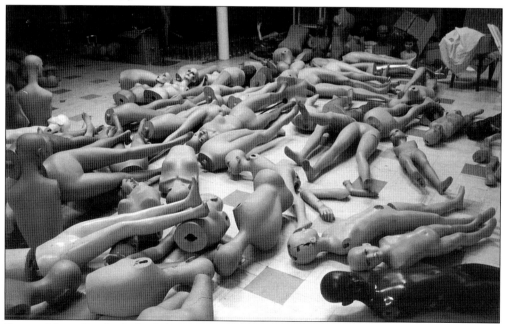

During Meyer Brother's final days, many loyal employees with decades of dedicated service, literally cried. "I had my chance to be a buyer several times, but didn't want to be one, I just wanted to be the best saleswoman ever," said one teary-eyed employee who worked at the store for 50 years. The photograph above was taken at Meyer Brothers on March 14, 1987, the day before it closed. (Courtesy Joseph Pascalli, *The Mill Street Forward*.)

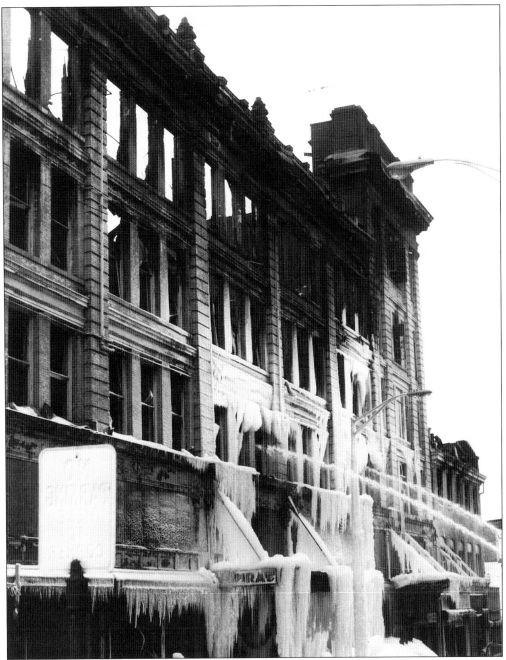

This is the chilling aftermath of the devastating 1991 fire that destroyed Meyer Brothers and much of three city blocks. As New Jersey Congressman Bill Pascrell Jr., a lifelong Patersonian, recalls: "I can remember going there with my mother as a boy into the beautiful elevator with the old ladies who operated them, feeling like they were bringing me closer to the heavens. When Meyer Brothers burned down, so did memories of quality service, memories of quality merchandise... There was no reason to go on the highway. The idea was not to look for the suburbs for direction, the idea was not to be like the suburbs, the idea was to value the city. There is pathos here." (Courtesy Mark Hillringhouse.)

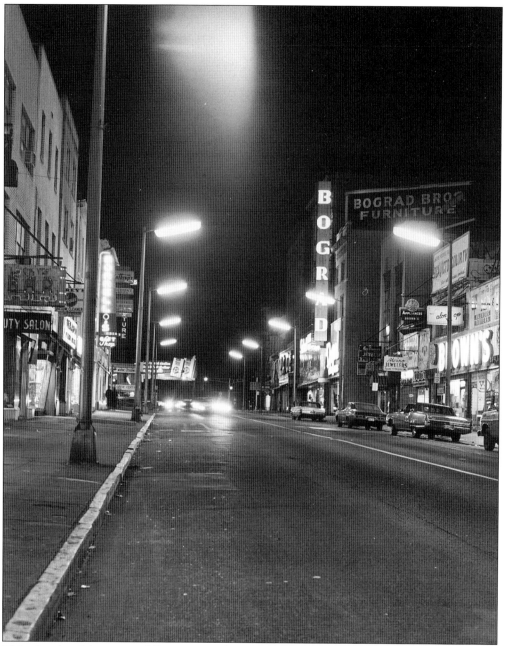

This ghostly night scene of Paterson in the 1970s depicts the desolate downtown nightlife that remains today. Since then, Bograd Brothers, a fine home furnishings store established in the 1930s, left the city for a suburban location. (By Michael R. Spozarsky, Courtesy Paterson Museum.)

Shown here is one of the many go-go-bars on Market Street that dominate the "entertainment scene" in downtown Paterson today. (Courtesy Tom Ufer.)

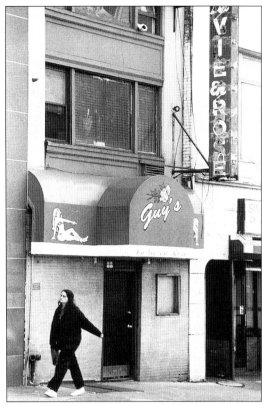

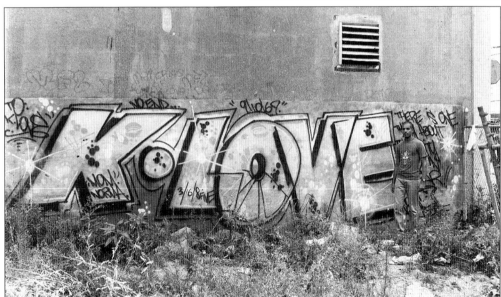

In 1987, Juan "Mitch" Santiago painted a memorial on East 18th Street for his deceased friend, Roberto "Tito" Rosa. The 17-year-old Patersonian was chased down by police on suspicion of selling drugs and shot in the head, during what the officer later described as an accidental shooting. The memorial, which still exists today, reads "K-Love," Tito's tagname, along with the epitaph: "There is one thing about this city: Fear." (Courtesy Ellen Denuto.)

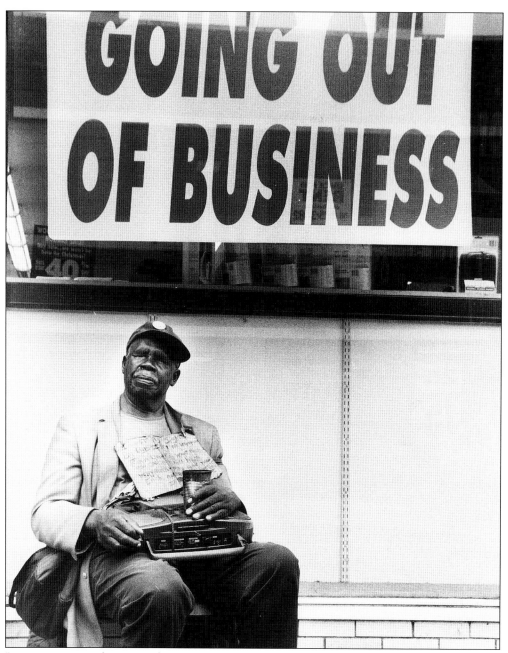

Be it in snow or glaring sunshine, James Bazemore has become a familiar sight to downtown shoppers at his spot in front of Woolworth's on Main Street for the past 25 years. His weather-worn sign reads: "I lost my sight by lye. I sell newspapers for a living. So whatever you can spare will help very much. May God Bless each and every one of you. In Jesus name. Amen." The classic five-and-dime store, which opened in 1912, closed its doors in 1998 with the distinction of being one of the last downtown buildings not to be covered with a plastic facade. The red and gold vintage sign of Woolworth's was taken down shortly after the store's closing. As for James, he remains in his favorite spot despite the iron gates. "I know the people here and the people know me," he says. (Courtesy Tom Ufer.)

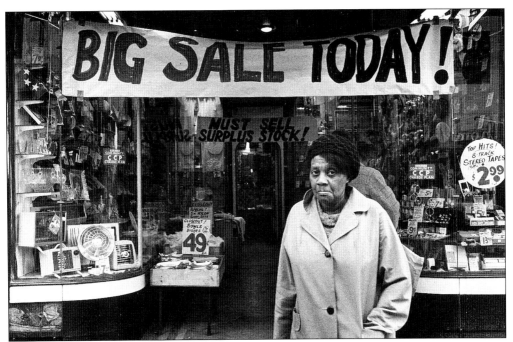

Main Street had changed considerably by the 1970s. (By Michael R. Spozarsky, Courtesy Paterson Museum.)

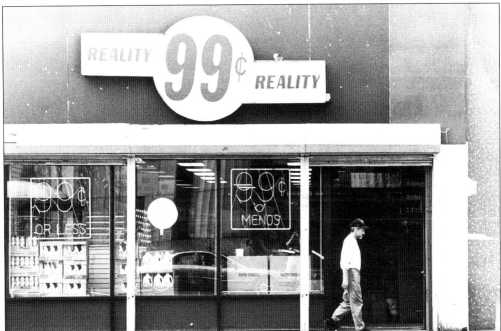

It seems to be the increasing reality of downtown stores in Paterson today to feature merchandise for under a buck, as this store does on Main Street. Do not confuse this store with "99¢ Dream" on Market Street or "99¢ Dreams" further up on Main! Bograd Brothers, a fine furniture store, was formerly located on the site that 99¢ Dreams currently occupies. (Courtesy Tom Ufer.)

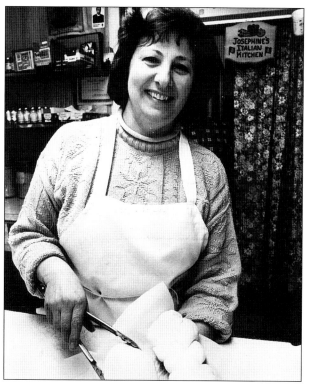

Josephine Grambone proudly holds up one of her beautiful homemade mozzarella's at Pantano's Dairy on the corner of Cianci and Passaic Streets. Josephine and her husband, Vincenzo, have owned the family-run deli for 23 years. Homemade cheeses, escarole, sausage rolls, and daily hot specials like her delicious lasagna are just a few of the culinary delights that can be found there. (By David Greedy, Courtesy *North Jersey Herald & News*.)

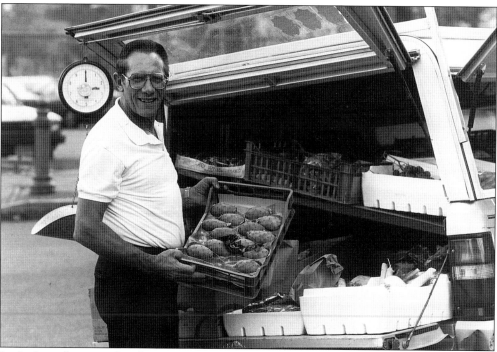

In the late afternoon, Serafino Di Gangi waits with his wagon for downtown factory and office workers, who buy his fresh fruits and vegetables on their way home. Serafino has been selling produce in the Paterson area since 1975. (Courtesy Ellen Denuto.)

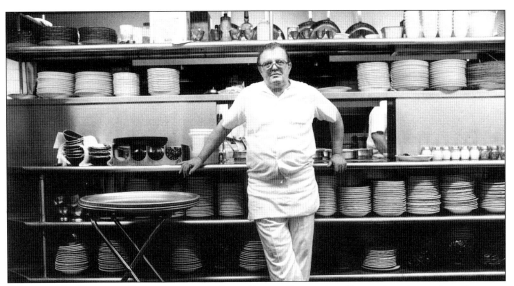

Owner of La Trattoria Restaurant on Ellison Street, Domenico Rocco immigrated to Paterson from Serino, Italy, in 1953. He began working at a dye house, but soon after switched to restaurants, where he discovered his love for cooking. La Trattoria is known for its tasty vodka sauce and large portions of pasta. Asked once why the servings are so generous, Domenico shrugged and joked: "The plates are big." *E vero*, the hand-painted plates, ordered from a friend in Salerno, Italy, are large. But who would argue with such delicious Patersonian reasoning anyway? (Courtesy Ellen Denuto.)

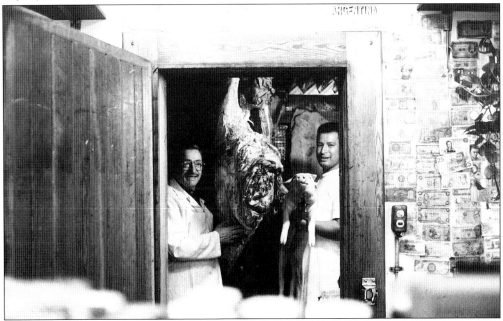

Carlos Tana and his assistant, Jorge Dela Cruz, are shown here at Tana's Food Market on Cianci Street. Carlos says he was after adventure when he came to America from Argentina with his wife, Perla, in 1958. Known by patrons for his talkative nature, Carlos is proud of his meat specialties, like *matambre*, a flank meat prepared with parsley, carrots, eggs, and garlic. (Courtesy Ellen Denuto.)

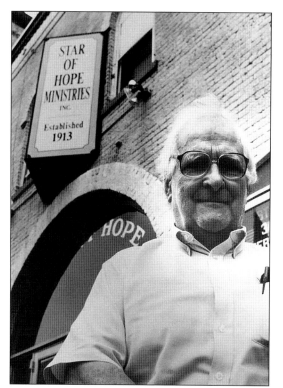

Customers of the Star of Hope Mission's unbeatable thrift shop know Francis Grimes for his lovable, cantankerous nature. From his seat by the door, the feisty watchman calls out playful, albeit sarcastic, comments and occasionally bursts into perverse lines of songs, like "It's Apple Picking Time in Paterson." Established on Broadway in 1913, the Star of Hope develops relationships between Paterson churches and volunteers, while helping to distribute goods that meet basic human needs. (By John Munson, Courtesy *North Jersey Herald & News*.)

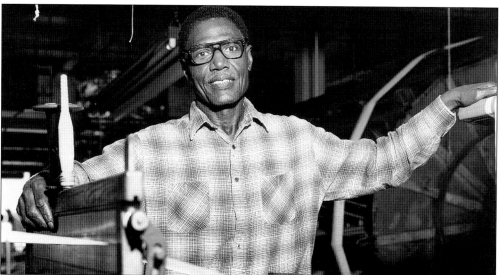

Expert warper Lonnie Stephenson once owned River Warping at 2 Broadway. After arriving from North Carolina in 1946, Lonnie learned all stages of the silk business from Abe Fricths and bought his business in 1961. In 1996, the Broadway building, established as the Vlaanderen Machine Company in 1899, was sold by Glenro, Inc., to a social service agency to house mentally and physically disabled families. Lonnie moved his business, now Eastside Warping, to Lindbergh Place, making his the last silk mill to leave the Historic District. "When you do something well, you do it well because you love to do it," says one of Paterson's last silk workers. (Courtesy Giacomo De Stefano.)

On any given day of the week, Walter Forbes, a retired garbage truck driver, can be seen in his straw Panama fishing hat waving and chatting to people who walk by the senior housing complex where he lives on Ellison Street. "You got to learn to take things slow and enjoy life," says Walter, relaxing here in his apartment with one of his pet cockateels, Jekyl. (Courtesy Ellen Denuto.)

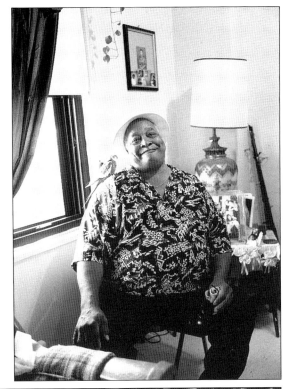

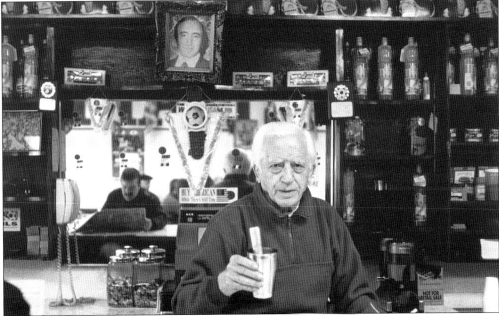

The making of a foamy, perfected cappuccino or a rich espresso is a tradition taken seriously by the many coffee and sports bars downtown. Frank Marianacci has been making first-rate cappuccinos for decades at the Roma Club on Cianci Street. Unlike more posh, assembly-line coffee houses out of town, here the authentic ambrosia can be purchased for only $1.25! (Courtesy Ellen Denuto.)

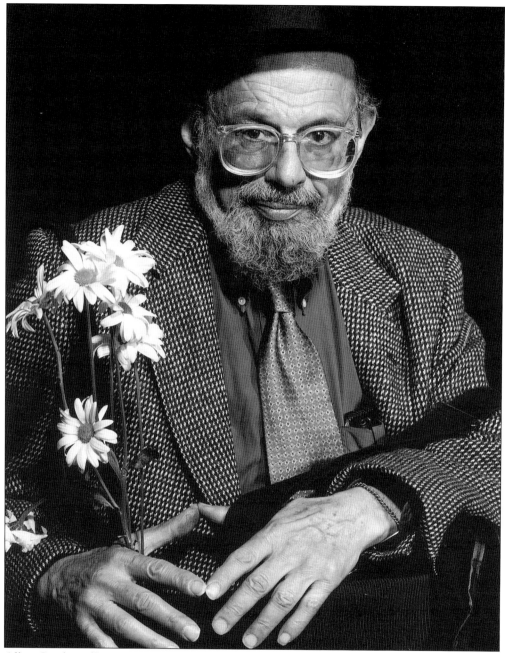

Allen Ginsberg (June 3, 1926–April 5, 1997), the internationally acclaimed poet, grew up on Fair Street. (Courtesy Giacomo De Stefano.)

Magic Spell

There once was a boy who lived in a wooden house uphill from the red brick mills along the Passaic River in Paterson, New Jersey, near the Great Falls. He was lonely and wandered over the concrete bridge above the raceway where purple water spilled from the silk-dye works into a pool where naked boys swam in summer heat sunny afternoons between the factory walls.

His friend Earl up the block protected him from bullies who slapped little kids without clothes and threatened to push them off the concrete edge of the swimming place on one end overlooking a rusty scrapyard filled with old cars.

He wished he had a Magic Spell and was King in ermine robes with gold crown, so that he could make Earl his Grand Wizard. He lost track of his protector Earl after he got out of Grammar School.

He grew up and went to India and studied Magic Spells. He sang *Hare Krishna Krishna Krishna Krishna Hare Hare Hare Rama Hare Rama Rama Rama Rama Hare Hare** for several years for protection. Then he sang *Om Namah Shivaye.*** That got him excited and everyone who heard him sang along, excited. Everyone got high, and then went home. But to get excited they had to sing the Magic Spell over and over. Then they got tired of being excited.

He grew older, and found it bothersome to sing long Magic Spells all the time, even though the new one he sang, *Gate Gate Paragate Parasamgate Bodhi Svaha,**** had a snappy rhythm and meant that no one had to get excited anymore, they could relax. Still, it was long and sounded mysterious.

War came and he went around singing a new Magic Spell that was easy to remember. When the tear gas drifted by in city parks and young, long-haired boys and girls yelled at policemen trying to chase them away, he walked around singing *OM* as loud as he could. That was okay, but it still sounded mysterious and though everyone knew it was a Magic Spell, nobody knew exactly what it meant.

War ended and he said *Ah*. That was it. It was a natural Magic Spell, everyone understood, saying *Ah*, just like Fourth of July appreciating fireworks. His beard grew white and he looked like a wise king and said *Ah* at every opportunity.

Ah was like a breath of air. In fact, you had to breath out to say it, and he was breathing all the time just like everyone else. One day he stopped saying *Ah*, but kept on breathing out. He discovered he was aware of the Magic Spell every few minutes just by breathing out. Other people were breathing but they weren't aware of the Magic Spell in their breathing most of the time, only sometimes when they remembered they were breathing out into space.

So he went around and looked people in the eyes, aware that he was breathing. They all treated him as if he were a king anyway, so he didn't need a crown or a robe. In bald middle age he asked advice from everyone he met so he found many Grand Wizards and they all helped rule the Earth.

He settled in New York City. Sometimes he goes to Paterson, New Jersey, and visits the pool between the factories. He stands silent there and breathes.

*Sing-song to the Preserver of the universe.
**Sing-song to the Changer of the universe.
***Gone out, Gone out, All gone out, All over gone, Wake Mind, so *Ah*.

—By Allen Ginsberg
Reprinted with permission of the Allen Ginsberg Trust, New York.

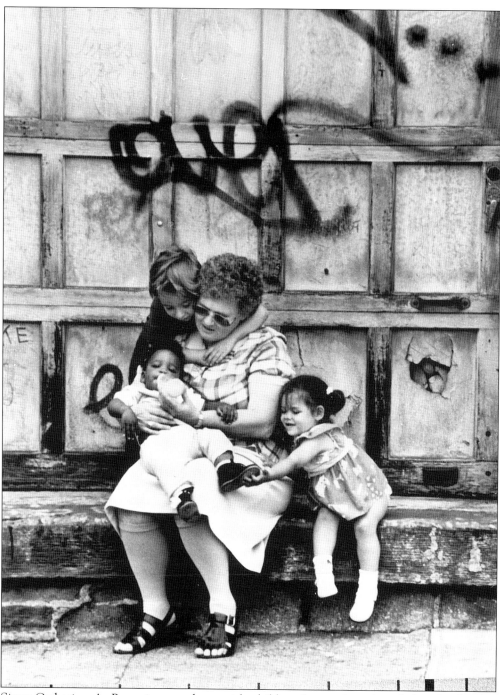
Sister Catherine A. Rowe is seen above with children from a homeless shelter for families located on Cianci Street. Sister Cathy, known and respected as a hands-on activist for the city's urban poor, died in 1991. (By Al Paglione, Courtesy *The Record*.)

Who restricts knowledge? Some say
it is the decay of the middle class
making an impossible moat between the high
and the low where
the life once flourished . . knowledge
of the avenues of information—
So that we do not know (in time)
where the stasis lodges. And if it is not
the knowledgeable idiots, the university,
they at least are the non-purveyors
should be devising means
to leap the gap. Inlets? The outward
masks of the special interests
that perpetuate the stasis and make it
profitable.

    They block the release
that should cleanse and assume
prerogatives as a private recompense.
Others are also at fault because
they do nothing.

—William Carlos Williams, from *Paterson*.
Excerpt from *The Delineaments of Giants, III*.
Copyright 1946, 1948, 1951 by William Carlos Williams.
Reprinted by permission of New Directions Publishing Corp., NY.

Acknowledgments

There are many people who made this book possible, through both their physical contributions and moral support. I would like to thank the writers who contributed their essays and poetry to this publication with a spirit of belief that was genuinely refreshing. Heartfelt appreciation to Passaic County Historian Edward A. Smyk for his undying wit and deep knowledge of Paterson history, the rare kind that can only be cultivated through an earnest mixture of scholarship and integrity. Thanks to Steve Golin, author and history professor at Bloomfield College, whose quintessential book *The Fragile Bridge: Paterson Silk Strike 1913* (Temple University Press) remains the kind of work that provides tangible food for the spirit, and one that I relied on for labor history while putting together this publication. I would like to thank Mark Hillringhouse for his beautiful poetry, my intelligent neighbor Candace Pryor for reminding me to remain serious about having fun, and Tom Carroll DeBlasio, a quality folklorist and, in general, good friend with great brains.

There are others whose words are used in this publication, adding insights about Paterson that possess depth of spirit. Some required the generous permissions of authors and publishers, while others were derived from people during interviews in the Paterson area or sent to me in written form in the past during my stint as editor of the *Mill Street Forward*. Special thanks to the people at Arcadia, especially Amy Sutton and Michael Joseph Guillory.

The support of the Paterson Museum to this publication was invaluable on two levels. While I would like to thank Paterson Museum Director Giacomo De Stefano and Christian Grube for their photographic expertise, and staff members Bruce Balistrieri and Robert Veronelli for their general assistance, the bulk of archival photographs used in this book were selected from the Paterson Museum collection. Most of the labor photographs in this publication were borrowed from the American Labor Museum in Haledon, and I would like to thank Director Angelica Santomauro, Bunny Botto Kuiken, and that eternally spry labor guy Sol Stetin, for their kindness and help. I would like to thank Andrew Shick at the Passaic County Historical Society for use of archival photos, my friends Ellen Denuto and Tom Ufer for their wonderful images of present-day Paterson, and all the other artists and publications who donated the use of photographs as well. Warm thanks to Allan Rowe Kelly, who is truly my Auntie Mame, for his uplifting nature and talented eyes while helping me layout the pages of this book.

Two men have supported me during this project, as they help me in my life in general. One is my gentle and loving father, Americo Avignone, who worked many long hours at the Triborough Bridge while I was going to school in New York, providing me with the luxury-called time to read books. The other is Gregory Van Maanen, who continuously reminds me, by example, of the honor and freedom found through creative work. I would like to dedicate this publication to my grandmother, Filomena Mele, whose memories of the Old Country and the Bronx I love listening to, and whose heart is like an apple of gold in a picture of silver.

—June Avignone
Editor